Microsoft® Office Small Business Accounting 2006 Step by Step

Curtis Frye and John Pierce

PUBLISHED BY
Microsoft Press
A Division of Microsoft Corporation
One Microsoft Way
Redmond, Washington 98052-6399

Library of Congress Control Number: 2005931545
Printed and bound in the United States of America.

1 2 3 4 5 6 7 8 9 QWT 9 8 7 6 5

Distributed in Canada by H.B. Fenn and Company Ltd. A CIP catalogue record for this book is available from the British Library.

Microsoft Press books are available through booksellers and distributors worldwide. For further information about international editions, contact your local Microsoft Corporation office or contact Microsoft Press International directly at fax (425) 936-7329. Visit our Web site at www.microsoft.com/learning/. Send comments to *mspinput@microsoft.com*.

Microsoft, Excel, Microsoft Press, and Windows are either registered trademarks or trademarks of Microsoft Corporation in the United States and/or other countries. Other product and company names mentioned herein may be the trademarks of their respective owners.

The example companies, organizations, products, domain names, e-mail addresses, logos, people, places, and events depicted herein are fictitious. No association with any real company, organization, product, domain name, e-mail address, logo, person, place, or event is intended or should be inferred.

Acquisitions Editor: Juliana Aldous
Developmental Editor: Sandra Haynes
Project Editor: Valerie Woolley
Editorial and Production Services: Studioserv

Body Part No. X11-44974

Contents

Contents

Contents

Getting Help

Every effort has been made to ensure the accuracy of this book and the contents of its CD-ROM. If you run into problems, please contact the appropriate source for help and assistance.

Getting Help with This Book and Its CD-ROM

If your question or issue concerns the content of this book or its companion CD-ROM, please first search the online Microsoft Press Knowledge Base, which provides support information for known errors in or corrections to this book, at the following Web site:

www.microsoft.com/learning/support/

If you do not find your answer in the online Knowledge Base, send your comments or questions to Microsoft Learning Technical Support at:

mspinput@microsoft.com

Getting Help with Microsoft Office Small Business Accounting 2006

If your question is about Microsoft Office Small Business Accounting 2006, and not about the content of this Microsoft Press book, please search the Microsoft Help and Support Center or the Microsoft Knowledge Base at:

support.microsoft.com

In the United States, Microsoft software product support issues not covered by the Microsoft Knowledge Base are addressed by Microsoft Product Support Services. The Microsoft software support options available from Microsoft Product Support Services are listed at:

support.microsoft.com

Outside the United States, for support information specific to your location, please refer to the Worldwide Support menu on the Microsoft Help and Support Web site for the site specific to your country:

support.microsoft.com

Using the Book's CD-ROM

The CD-ROM inside the back cover of this book contains two additional chapters of material that didn't fit in the book but will help you use Microsoft Office Small Business Accounting 2006 effectively. This book's CD-ROM also includes valuable resources and downloads along with a selection of additional electronic books (eBooks) to help you get the most out of your Small Business Accounting experience.

Minimum System Requirements

To use this book, your computer should meet the following requirements:

- **Computer/Processor**   A computer with a Pentium 133-megahertz (MHz) or higher processor; 733-megahertz is recommended.

- **Memory**   128 MB of RAM; 256 MB is recommended.

- **Hard disk**   Hard disk space requirements vary depending on configuration; custom installation choices might require more or less hard disk space. For the ebooks and downloads, we recommend 250 MB of available hard disk space with 115 MB on the hard disk where the operating system is installed.

- **Operating System**   While you can use any Microsoft operating system, Microsoft Windows XP Professional Edition was used to capture all the screen shots.

- **Drive**   CD-ROM or DVD-ROM drive

- **Display**   Super VGA (800×600) or higher-resolution monitor with 256 colors

- **Software**   Internet Explorer 5.01 SP1 or later, Microsoft Office Word 2003, Microsoft Office Excel 2003, Microsoft Office Access 2003, Microsoft Office Outlook 2003, and Microsoft Office InfoPath 2003.

Opening the Practice Files

The exercises in *Microsoft Office Small Business Accounting 2006 Step By Step* use the two sample databases included when you install Microsoft Office Small Business Accounting 2006. Follow these steps to open a sample database:

1   Start Small Business Accounting.

2   In the **Start** dialog box, click **Open a Sample Company**.

3   In the **Select Sample Company** dialog box, select the option representing the type of sample file you want to open.

4   Click **OK**.

Using the Practice Files

Each exercise is preceded by a paragraph or paragraphs that list the sample company file needed for that exercise and explain any preparation you need to take care of before you start working through the exercise, as shown here:

OPEN the Fabrikam sample file.

Wherever possible, we made the exercises independent of each other. However, if you choose to do exercises in a sequence other than that presented in the book, be aware that there are exercises in some chapters that depend on other exercises performed earlier in the book. If this is the case, we will tell you where the prerequisite exercise is located in the book.

Reinstalling the Practice Files

If you would like to reinstall the Fabrikam or Northwind Traders sample company files, you can do so by following these steps:

1 Start Small Business Accounting.

2 If a company file is open, on the **File** menu, click **Close Company**.

The company file closes and the **Start** page appears.

3 Click **Delete a Company**.

The **Delete a Database** dialog box appears.

4 Click the database you would like to delete, and click the **Delete** button.

A verification dialog box appears.

5 Click **Yes**.

The dialog box disappears.

6 Click **Close**.

The **Delete a Database** dialog box disappears.

7 Click **Open a Sample Company**.

The **Select Sample Company** dialog box appears.

8 Select the option representing the sample company you want to open.

9 Click **OK**.

A new copy of the sample company file appears.

Conventions and Features

You can save time when you use this book by understanding how the *Step by Step* series shows special instructions, keys to press, buttons to click, and so on.

Convention	Meaning
1 **2**	Numbered steps guide you through hands-on exercises in each topic.
●	A round bullet indicates an exercise that has only one step.
Tip	These paragraphs provide a helpful hint or shortcut that makes working through a task easier.
Important	These paragraphs point out information that you need to know to complete the procedure.
Troubleshooting	These paragraphs show you how to fix a common problem that might prevent you from continuing with the exercise.
Alt + Tab	A plus sign (+) between two key names means that you must hold down the first key while you press the second key. For example, "Press Alt + Tab" means "hold down the Alt key while you press the Tab key."
Black bold characters	In steps, program features that you click or press are shown in black bold type.
Blue italic characters	Terms explained in the glossary are shown in blue italic type.
Blue bold characters	Text that you are supposed to type appears in blue bold type in the procedures.
Italic characters	Folder paths, URLs, and emphasized words appear in italic type.
BE SURE TO	These words are found at the beginning of paragraphs preceding or following step-by-step exercises. They point out items you should check or actions you should carry out either before beginning an exercise or after completing an exercise.

Convention	Meaning
USE OPEN	These words are found at the beginning of paragraphs preceding step-by-step exercises. They draw your attention to practice files that you'll need to use in the exercise.
CLOSE	This word is found at the beginning of paragraphs following step-by-step exercises. They give instructions for closing open files or programs before moving on to another topic.

Quick Reference

Setting Up a New Company

To view a sample company file

1 In the Start dialog box, click Open a Sample Company.

2 In the Select Sample Company dialog box, select either the Service Based Sample Company option or the Product Based Sample Company option.

3 Click OK.

To create a new company file

1 In the Start dialog box, click Set Up Your Company to launch the Startup Wizard.

2 Read the information on the Company and Preferences wizard page, gather the information the wizard recommends that you collect, and then click Next to display the Company Details Introduction wizard page.

3 Click Next to display the Add Company Details wizard page.

4 Type your company's information in the fields on the Add Company Details wizard page.

5 Click Next to display the Set Up Accounts wizard page.

6 Select the Select Your Business Type and Have Small Business Accounting Suggest Accounts option to have the program create standard accounts for your business.

7 Click Next to display the Set Up Accounts (Cont.) wizard page.

8 Click the Business Type down arrow and select the business type that best describes your business.

9 Click Next to display the Select a Fiscal Year and Start Date wizard page.

10 In the Beginning of the First Fiscal Year field, type the first day of your company's first fiscal year.

11 In the End of the First Fiscal Year field, type the last day of your company's first fiscal year.

12 In the Start Date field, type the first day for which you will enter transactions.

13 Click Next, read the information on the Preferences introduction page, and then click Next again to display the Select Jobs Preferences wizard page.

14 Select the Yes option if you want to track jobs in Small Business Accounting, or select the No option if you don't want to track jobs.

15 Click Next to display the Select Sales Tax Preferences wizard page.

16 If your company collects sales tax, select the Yes option. If your company doesn't collect sales tax, or if you don't know your sales tax rates, select the No option.

17 Click Next.

18 If you selected the I Collect a Single Tax Rate and Pay It to a Single Tax Agency option on the previous wizard page, the Select Sales Tax Preferences (Cont.) wizard page appears. In the fields provided, type in a name for the tax, the tax rate, and the name of the agency to which you pay the tax, and click Next

19 On the Select Form Layout Preference wizard page, select the Sells Services option if your company only sells services; otherwise, select the Sells Products, or Both Products and Services option.

20 Click Next to display the Select Numbering Preferences wizard page.

21 Select the check boxes next to the types of accounts to which you want Small Business Accounting to assign a unique identifying number.

22 Click Next to display the Set Up Payroll wizard page.

23 If you plan to use the ADP Payroll for Small Business Accounting service, select the Yes option to have the program remind you to set up your payroll process after you close the wizard. If not, select the No option.

24 Click Next.

25 If you want to change any of your settings, click the Back button to revisit your selections. When you're done, click Finish.

26 In the File Name field, type your company's name and then click Save.

16 **To change your company preferences**

1 On the Company menu, click Preferences.

2 The Company Preferences dialog box appears.

3 Use the controls in the Company Preferences dialog box to set or change your company preferences.

4 Click OK to save your changes.

17 **To import data from a Small Business Accounting XML file**

1 On the File menu, point to Utilities and then click Import.

2 In the Import Data dialog box, make sure Microsoft Office Small Business Accounting Data is selected, and click OK.

3 Click Browse.

4 In the Select a File to Import From dialog box, navigate to the directory that contains the XML file you want to import, click the file name, and then click Open.

5   Click Import.

6   Click OK to dismiss the results dialog box.

17   **To import company data from QuickBooks**

1   In the Start dialog box, click Import Data from QuickBooks.

2   Read the information on the Introduction wizard page and click Next.

3   Type your company's information into the fields on the Company Contact Details wizard page.

4   Click Next to display the Select a Fiscal Year and Start Date wizard page.

5   In the Beginning of the First Fiscal Year field, type the first day of your company's first fiscal year.

6   In the End of the First Fiscal Year field, type the last day of your company's first fiscal year.

7   In the Start Date field, type the first day for which you will enter transactions.

8   Click Next to pass the Instructions for Migration page.

9   ˙Click Next to display the Select QuickBooks Master Records wizard page.

10   Clear the check box next to any data type you do not want to migrate to Small Business Accounting.

11   If the file you want to migrate doesn't appear in the File to Import From field, click the Browse button, use the Select File dialog box to locate the file you want to migrate, and click Open.

12   Click Next.

13   Click Import.

14   Use the controls in the Save Company dialog box to define a name and save location for your new corporate data file.

15   Click Save.

16   Click Finish to close the Data Migration Wizard and display the company data you imported.

19   **To export company data**

1   On the File menu, point to Utilities, and then click Export.

2   The Export Data dialog box appears.

3   In the Export Data dialog box, click Browse.

4   In the Select a File to Export to dialog box, either click a file to export data to an existing file or type a file name to export data to a new file.

5 Click Save.

6 In the Pick a File to Export to dialog box, under Data to Export, select the check boxes next to the data you want to export.

7 Click Export.

8 Click OK to dismiss the confirmation dialog box.

9 Click Close to dismiss the Export Data dialog box.

22 **Creating a backup file**

1 On the File menu, point to Utilities and then click Data Utilities.

2 If necessary, in the Small Business Accounting Data Tools dialog box, click the Basic Tools tab.

3 Click Backup.

4 In the Create a Backup File dialog box, click Browse.

5 In the Backup dialog box, click the file you want to replace or type a name for the file in the File Name field.

6 Click Save.

7 If desired, type a password for the file in the Password field and then type the same password in the Verify Password field.

8 Click OK.

9 Click OK to dismiss the confirmation dialog box that appears.

10 Click Close.

23 **To restore data from a backup file**

1 On the File menu, point to Utilities, and then click Data Utilities.

2 If necessary, in the Small Business Accounting Data Tools dialog box, click the Basic Tools tab.

3 Click Restore.

4 In the Database Restore dialog box, click the Browse button to the right of the Backup Filename field.

5 In the Restore dialog box, click the file you want to restore and click Open.

6 Click the Browse button to the right of the Restore Backup File To field.

7 In the Select Configuration File dialog box, click the file you want to overwrite or type the name of a new file in the File Name field.

8 Click Save.

9 If the file is password protected, type its password in the Password field.

10 Click OK.

11 Click OK to dismiss the Restore Complete dialog box.

12 Click Close.

25 **To create a new user account**

1 On the File menu, click Manage Users.

2 In the Manage Users dialog box, click Select.

3 In the Select Small Business Accounting User wizard, click Select User.

4 In the Select User dialog box, in the Enter the Object Name to Select field, type the name of the user for whom you want to create a new account.

5 Click Check Names.

6 Click OK.

7 Click Next.

8 Click the User Role down arrow and select the role you want to assign to the selected user.

9 Click Finish.

28 **To delete a user account**

1 On the File menu, click Manage Users.

2 In the Manage Users dialog box, in the Users Who Have Access to This Application list, click the user account you want to delete.

3 Click Remove.

4 Click OK to verify that you want to delete the account.

5 Click Close.

Chapter 3 Managing the Chart of Accounts and Journal Entries List

Page 32 **To view the Chart of Accounts**

1 In the Navigation pane, click Company or Banking.

2 Under Find, click Chart of Accounts.

37 **To manipulate the Chart of Accounts**

1 In the Navigation pane, click Company.

2 Under Find, click Chart of Accounts.

3 On the View menu, click Add/Remove Content.

4 In the Grid Customization dialog box, click a column heading you want to add in the Available Column Headings list, and then click Add.

5 To change the order in which the columns appear, click the column you want to move in the Show Columns in This Order list, and then click the Move Up or Move Down button.

6 To remove a column from the chart of accounts, click the column heading in the Show Columns in This Order list, and then click Remove.

7 To filter the account list, open the Current View list at the top right of the chart of accounts, and then click Active, Inactive, or All.

38 **To create a new account**

1 In the Navigation pane, click Company.

2 Under Start a Task, click New Account.

3 In the Select Account Type dialog box, select the type of account you want to add, and then click OK.

4 In the account form, type an account number in the Account no. box.

5 In the Account name box, type a descriptive name for the account.

6 Type the account's opening balance, if any, in the Balance field.

7 In the Subaccount of list, select the account the new account contributes to.

8 In the Cash Flow Category list, select the appropriate category from among Operating, Investing, and Financing.

9 In the 1099 Category list, select the category that is appropriate for this account.

10 In the Comments box, type information about how to use an account.

11 Click Save and Close.

41 **To edit an account**

1 In the Navigation pane, click Company.

2 Under Find, click Chart of Accounts.

3 Right-click the account you want to edit and then click Open Selected Items.

4 Use the controls in the dialog box to edit the account.

5 On the toolbar, click Save and Close.

42 **To merge two accounts**

1 On the Company menu, point to Merge Accounts, and then click Merge Financial Accounts.

2 In the Merge Financial Accounts dialog box , under Merge From, in the Merge from Account list, click the account you want to merge from.

3 Under Merge Into, in the Merge to Account list, click the account into which you will incorporate the records.

4 Click OK.

44 **Add a journal entry**

1 In the Navigation pane, click Company.

2 Under Start a Task, click New Journal Entry.

3 In the Memo box, type text to describe the purpose of the journal entry.

4 In the Voucher No. box, keep the number 1.

5 In the Type column, select the type of account to which you want to add a journal entry.

6 In the Account column, click the desired account.

7 In the Memo box, type additional information about each entry.

8 In the Credit column, type the value of the credit to be applied.

9 Press TAB until you create a new entry row in the journal.

10 Create an entry for an account to balance the credit (e.g., if you sold a parcel of land for $65,000, you would credit $65,000 to the Land account and debit $65,000 into one of your bank accounts).

11 On the toolbar, click Save and Close.

47 **To view the account register of an account**

1 In the Navigation pane, click Company.

2 Under Find, click Chart of Accounts.

3 In the chart of accounts, double-click the account you want to view.

49 **To edit a journal entry**

1 In the Navigation pane, click Company.

2 Under Find, click Journal Entries.

3 Double-click the journal entry you want to edit.

4 On the toolbar, click Edit.

5 Change the information on the journal entry form.

6 On the toolbar, click Save and Close.

50 **To void a journal entry**

1 In the Navigation pane, click Company.

2 Under Find, click Journal Entries.

3   Double-click the journal entry you want to void.

4   On the Actions menu, click Void.

5   To confirm that you want to void the entry, click Yes.

6   Click Save and Close.

Chapter 4   Managing Products and Services

To view the Item List

●   On the Company menu, point to Company Lists, and click Items.

To change the items displayed in a list

●   Click the Current View down arrow and then click the items you want to view.

To sort a list by the values in a column

1   Click a column header once to sort the list in ascending order based on the column's values.

2   Click the column header again to sorts the list in descending order.

3   Click the column header again to return the column to its unsorted state.

To filter a list

1   Display the list you want to view.

2   On the Actions menu, click Find.

3   On the Find toolbar, in the Look For field, type the term by which you want to filter the list.

4   Click the Search Under down arrow and select the field by which you want to filter the list.

5   Click Find.

6   Click Clear.

7   On the Find toolbar, click the Close button to hide the Find toolbar.

To create a new item

1   On the toolbar, click the New button down arrow, and then click New Item.

2   The Select Item Type dialog box appears.

3   Select the option representing the type of item you want to create.

4   Click OK.

5   In the dialog box that appears, fill in the details for the item.

6   Click Save and Close.

60 **To add custom fields to a form**

1   Click the Custom Fields tab.

2   The Custom Fields tab page appears.

3   On the Custom Fields tab page, click Customize.

4   In the Customize Form dialog box, select the check box in the Display column next to the first row that contains Date in the Field Type column.

5   Press the TAB key.

6   In he Field Name field, type a name for the field and click OK.

7   Click Save and Close.

61 **To change the quantity of an inventory item**

1   On the Vendors menu, point to Adjust Inventory, and then click Adjust Quantity.

2   In the Adjust Inventory Quantity dialog box, click the Adjustment Account down arrow, and then click the account to which you want to assign the cost of the adjustment.

3   On the row of the Inventory Items list that represents the item you want to adjust, click in the Qty. Difference field.

4   Type a value by which to adjust the quantity and press TAB.

5   Click Save and Close.

62 **Adjusting the quantity and value of an inventory item**

1   On the Vendors menu, point to Adjust Inventory, and then click Adjust Quantity and Value.

2   In the Adjust Inventory Quantity and Value dialog box, click the Adjustment Account down arrow, and then click Cost of Goods – Materials.

3   In the Inventory Items list, on the row of the item you want to change, click in the New Quantity field.

4   Type the new quantity.

5   On the same row, click in the Current Value field.

6   Type a new value for the item and press TAB.

7   Click Save and Close.

63 **To create a new service item**

1   On the toolbar, click the New button down arrow, and then click New Item.

2   In the Select Item Type dialog box appears, select the Service option.

3   Click OK.

4   In the Untitled – Service Item dialog box appears, in the Item Name field, type a name for the item.

5   Click the Item Group down arrow, and then click the group to which you want to add the item.

6   In the Sales Description field, type a description.

7   In the Sales Price field, type a price.

8   Click the Income Account down arrow, and then click the desired income account.

9   In the Standard Cost field, type the standard cost.

10   Click Save and Close.

64 **To change a service item's price**

1   On the Vendors menu, click Change Item Prices.

2   In the Change Item Price dialog box, select the check boxes next to the items you want to change.

3   Under Price Change, select the Percentage option.

4   In the Percentage field, type the percentage by which you want to change the price.

5   Click Calculate.

6   Click OK.

66 **Change the status of an item**

1   On the Company menu, point to Company Lists and then click Items.

2   On the Item List, click the Current View down arrow and then click the status of the items you want to display.

3   Right-click the item you want to change and then click the status you want to assign to the item.

67 **To delete an item**

1   On the Company menu, point to Company Lists and then click Items.

2   On the Item List, click the item you want to delete.

3   On the toolbar, click the Delete button, then click Yes to confirm the deletion.

68 **To create a custom group**

1   On the Company menu, point to Manage Support Lists, and then click Item Group List.

2   In the Modify Item Groups dialog box, click Add.

3 In the Add or Edit Item Group Name dialog box, in the Item Group Name field, type a name for the group.

4 Click OK.

68 **To edit a custom group**

1 On the Company menu, point to Manage Support Lists, and then click Item Group List.

2 In the Modify Item Groups dialog box, if necessary, click the name of the group.

3 Click Edit.

4 In the Add or Edit Item Group Name dialog box, in the Item Group Name field, type a new name for the group.

5 Click OK.

6 Click Close.

Chapter 5 Setting Up Customer Information

Page 75 **Create a customer record**

1 On the Navigation pane, click Customers.

2 Under More Tasks, click New Customer.

3 In the Customer Name box, type the customer's name.

4 In the appropriate fields of the Address dialog box, type the customer's business address.

5 Click the Addresses down arrow, click Ship To, and then type the customer's shipping address.

6 Under Phone and Fax Numbers, type your customer's phone numbers.

7 In the Fax field, type the customer's fax number.

8 In the Customer Since field, if necessary, change the date to the date you took on the customer.

9 Under Contacts, click in the Contact Name field, type in the customer's name, and then fill in the other fields.

10 Click Save and Close.

81 **To create a new customer group**

1 On the Company menu, point to Manage Support Lists, and then click Customer Group List.

2 In the Modify Customer Group dialog box, click Add.

3   In the Customer Group dialog box, type a name for the group, and click OK.

4   Click Close.

84 **To create a price level**

1   On the Company menu, point to Manage Support Lists, and then click Price Level List.

2   In the Modify Price Level dialog box, click Add.

3   In the Add or Edit Price Level dialog box, in the Price Level field, type the name of the new group.

4   In the Percentage field, type the percentage by which you want to adjust these customers' prices.

5   Verify that the correct option (to increase or decrease prices) is selected.

6   Click OK, and then click Close in the Modify Price Level dialog box.

84 **To define a new credit rating**

1   On the Company menu, point to Manage Support Lists, and then click Credit Rating List.

2   In the Modify Credit Rating dialog box, click Add.

3   In the Credit Rating dialog box, type the name of the new credit rating.

4   In the Credit Rating dialog box, click OK, and then click Close in the Modify Credit Rating dialog box.

85 **To create a new payment term**

1   On the Company menu, point to Manage Support Lists, and then click Payment Terms List.

2   In the Modify Payment Term dialog box, click Add.

3   In the top portion of the Payment Term dialog box, type the name of the payment term. Then, in the Description box, type a description for the term.

4   In the Due boxes, type the number of days after which the payment is due.

5   In the Cash Discount area of the Payment Term dialog box, type the discount and enter the number of days within which the customer must pay to earn that discount.

6   In the Payment Term dialog box, click OK, and then click Close in the Modify Payment Term dialog box.

87 **To define a new tax agency**

1   On the Company menu, point to Sales Tax, and then click New Tax Agency.

2   In the Tax Agency box, type the name of the tax agency.

3 Under Account Information, in the Payment Term list, click the interval at which tax payments are due.

4 In the Liability Account list, click Sales Tax Payable.

5 Complete the contact information you want to enter for the tax agency, and then click Save and Close.

88 **To create a sales tax code**

1 On the Company menu, point to Sales Tax, and then click Manage Sales Tax Codes.

2 In the Manage Tax Code Name dialog box, click Add.

3 In the Add or Edit Tax Code dialog box, in the Tax Code box, type the name of the tax code.

4 In the Tax Agency list, click the agency to which you want to assign the code.

5 In the Tax Settings: Rate area, type the percentage rate of the tax. Then, in the As Of field, type the date as of which the tax is effective.

6 In the Add or Edit Tax Code dialog box, click OK, and then click Close in the Modify Tax Code Name dialog box.

89 **To create a sales tax group**

1 On the Company menu, point to Sales Tax, and then click Manage Sales Tax Groups.

2 In the Modify Sales Tax Group dialog box, click Add.

3 In the Tax Group dialog box, in the Selected Tax Group box, type the name of the group.

4 In the Available Tax Codes list, click the tax code you want to add to the group and then click Add. If more than one new tax applies to the group, you can repeat this step to add any other applicable tax codes.

5 Click OK, and then click Close in the Modify Sales Tax Group dialog box.

91 **To add details to a customer record**

1 On the Customers menu, point to Customer Lists, and then click Customers.

2 In the Customer List, double-click the customer you want to edit, and then click the Details tab.

3 Use the controls on the Details tab to change the customer's record.

4 Click Save and Close.

94 **To create a Microsoft Word template**

1 On the Company menu, click Manage Word Templates.

2 In the Template Types list, click the template category you want to use, and then click Create.

3   In the Create New Microsoft Word Template dialog box, type the name of the new template.

4   Click Create.

5   In the Document Actions task pane, ensure that the Show XML Tags in the Document check box is selected.

6   Click the first field you want to add.

7   Click to the right of the closing XML tag.

8   In the Document Actions task pane, click the other fields you want to add.

9   In Word, on the File menu, click Save.

10   In Word, on the File menu, click Exit.

Chapter 6   Managing Jobs

Page 102   **To display the Job List**

●   On the Company menu, point to Company Lists and then click Jobs.

107   **To display a job's details**

1   On the Customers menu, click Customers Home.

2   In the Find section at the bottom of the Customers page, click Jobs.

3   Scroll through the Jobs List and double-click the job you want to display.

4   Click the Financial History tab.

5   On the job window's toolbar, click Save and Close.

108   **To create a job**

1   On the Customers menu, click Customers Home.

2   In the More Tasks section of the Customers page, click New Job to open a blank Job form.

3   Fill in the job's details in the form.

4   On the toolbar, click the Save and Close button.

110   **To edit a job**

1   On the Customers menu, point to Customers Lists and then click Jobs.

2   In the Job List, double-click the job you want to edit.

3   Change the information you want to edit.

4   Click Save and Close.

Chapter 7 Generating and Managing Quotes

7   Click the Price Level down arrow, and then click the price level.

8   On the Sales Order form toolbar, click the Save and Close button.

135   **To create a sales order from a quote**

1   On the Customers menu, click Customers Home.

2   In the Start a Task section of the Customers home page, click New Sales Order.

3   On the sales order toolbar, click the Create From button.

4   In the Select a Quote dialog box, click the desired quote.

5   Click OK.

6   Click Save and Close.

141   **To edit a sales order**

1   On the Customers menu, point to Customer Lists, and then click Sales Orders.

2   In the Sales Order List, double-click the sales order.

3   Change the terms of the sales order.

4   Click Save and Close.

142   **To remind you of items on back order**

1   If necessary, in the Navigation Pane, click Company.

2   At the bottom right corner of the Today's Reminders section, click the Add/Remove button.

3   In the Add/Remove Reminders dialog box, select the Back Orders check box.

4   Click OK.

Chapter 9   Preparing and Managing Invoices

147   **To create an invoice from scratch**

1   On the Customers menu, point to New, and then click New Invoice.

2   Click the Customer Name down arrow, and then click the customer name.

3   Fill in the Payment terms and Delivery Date fields.

4   Under Products and Services, click in the Name column for the first row, click the down arrow, and then click the first item.

5   In the active line item, fill in the Qty. (Quantity) field.

6   If desired, type a discount percentage in the Discount field.

7   Click the Save and Close button on the toolbar.

150 **Create a progress invoice from a quote**

1 On the Customers menu, point to New, and then click New Invoice.

2 On the Invoice form toolbar, click Create from.

3 In the Create From dialog box, click quote number from which you want to create the progress invoice.

4 In the Percentage of Quote box, type the percentage to bill.

5 Click OK.

6 On the Invoice form toolbar, click Save and Close.

151 **To create an invoice from a job**

1 On the Navigation pane, under Find, click Jobs.

2 In the Job List, click the job from which you want to create the invoice.

3 On the Actions menu, click New Invoice for Job.

4 On the Invoice form toolbar, click Job Costs.

5 In the Time and Materials dialog box, click the Items tab.

6 Clear the check boxes for items you don't want to bill for.

7 Click OK.

8 Click Save and Close.

153 **To void an invoice**

1 In the Navigation pane, click Customers.

2 Under Find, click Invoices.

3 In the invoice list, double-click the invoice you want to void.

4 On the Actions menu, click Void, and then click Yes in the message box.

5 On the toolbar, click Save and Close.

154 **To edit a voided invoice**

1 In the Navigation pane, click Customers.

2 Under Find, click Invoices.

3 In the Current View box at the top right of the invoice list, click Voided.

4 In the list of voided invoices, double-click the invoice to edit.

5 On the File menu, click Copy and Edit.

6 Edit the invoice.

To record a finance charge

1   In the Navigation pane, click Customers.

2   Under Start a Task, click Finance Charge.

3   In the Finance Charge form, clear the check boxes on the rows representing customers to whom you don't want to apply a finance charge.

4   On the toolbar, click Save and Close.

Chapter 10   Handling Customer Payments

Receive a payment into Small Business Accounting

1   On the Customers menu, click Receive Payment.

2   In the unnamed date field at the top right corner of the Customer Payment form, type the date of the payment.

3   Click the Received from down arrow, and then click the customer from whom you received the payment.

4   In the Amount field, type the amount you received.

5   Click the Deposit in down arrow, and then click the account to which you want to deposit the funds you received.

6   Click Save and Close.

Void a payment

1   On the Customers menu, point to Customer Lists, and then click Payments.

2   Click the payment you want to void.

3   On the Actions menu, click Void and then click Yes to confirm the action.

To record a cash sale

1   On the Customers menu, point to New, and then click New Cash Sale.

2   Click the Customer Name down arrow and then click the customer's name.

3   On the first line of the Products and Services list, click in the Name field.

4   Click the down arrow that appears and then click the product sold.

5   Click Save and Close.

To sign up for credit card processing

1   On the Customers menu, point to Credit Card Processing and then click Sign Up for Credit Card Processing.

2   Under Establish a New Account, click the Learn More link.

3   Click the plan to which you want to subscribe and follow the directions in the wizard to sign up.

168 **To issue a refund by check**

1 On the Customers menu, point to New, and then click New Credit Memo.

2 Click the Customer Name down arrow, and then click the customer name.

3 In the Products and Services list, click in the Name column.

4 In the Name column, click the down arrow, and then click the first item.

5 On the File menu, click Save.

6 On the Customer Credit Memo form toolbar, click Check Refund.

7 In the untitled Check form, click the Bank Account down arrow, and then click Checking.

8 Click Save and Close.

169 **To issue a refund to a customer's credit card**

1 On the Customers menu, point to New, and then click New Credit Memo.

2 A blank Customer Credit Memo form appears.

3 In the Customer Credit Memo form, click the Customer Name down arrow, and then click the customer name.

4 In the Products and Services list, click in the first Name field.

5 Click the Name down arrow, and then click the first product.

6 In the Qty. field, type the quantity.

7 On the File menu, click Save.

8 On the Customer Credit Memo form toolbar, click Credit Card Refund.

9 Follow the instructions in the wizard to complete the refund.

171 **To create a credit memo from an invoice**

1 On the Customers menu, point to Customer Lists, and then click Invoices.

2 Click the invoice for which you want to create a credit memo.

3 On the Actions menu, click Create Credit Memo.

4 If necessary, in the Products and Services list, right-click the row header of an item you want to delete, and then click Delete.

5 If necessary, adjust values in the remaining rows' Qty. fields.

6 Click Save and Close.

Chapter 11 Purchasing from and Paying Vendors

11   In the Pay column, select the check box for each bill you want to pay.

12   Click Save and Close.

Chapter 12   Managing Employee Time and Payroll

To create a new employee record

1   On the Employees menu, click New Employee.

2   Fill in the employee's information in the Employee form.

3   Click Save and Close.

  To edit an employee record

4   On the Employees menu, point to Employee Lists and then click Employees.

5   In the Employee List, double-click the record you want to edit.

6   Change the values in the form.

7   Click Save and Close.

  To enter time by using a weekly time sheet

1   On the Employees menu, click New Timesheet.

2   In the untitled Weekly Timesheet window, in the Select Week field, type the first day of the week for which you want to enter time.

3   Click the Employee Name down arrow and then click the employee for whom you want to enter time.

4   If necessary, in the first row of the grid, select the Billable check box.

5   Click in the Customer field, click the down arrow that appears, and then click the customer for whom the employee did the work.

6   Press Tab.

7   Click the Billing Item down arrow and then click the job performed.

8   Repeat the previous step three times to record eight hours of work for Tuesday, Wednesday, and Thursday of the current week.

9   Click Save and Close.

  To create a time entry

1   On the Employees menu, point to Employee Lists and then click Time Entries.

2   Just below the Time Entry List headers, click Add a New Time Entry.

3   Fill in the details of the employee's time.

4   Click Save and Close.

Chapter 13 Managing Bank Accounts and Transactions

To add a transaction to a bank account

1 In the Navigation Pane, click Banking.

2 On the Banking menu, click Account Register.

3 In the Bank Account list, click the account to which you want to add the transaction.

4 At the bottom of the list of transactions, click the link Click Here to Add a New Transaction.

5 Fill in the transaction's details and then click OK.

To edit a transaction

1 In the Navigation Pane, click Banking.

2 On the Banking menu, click Account Register.

3 In the Bank Account list, click the account with the transaction you want to edit.

4 Double-click the transaction.

5 Change the values in the Debit and Credit columns to reflect the actual value of the transaction.

6 Click Save and Close.

To void a banking transaction

1 In the Navigation Pane, click Banking.

2 On the Banking menu, click Account Register.

3 In the Bank Account list, click the account with the transaction you want to edit.

4 Double-click the transaction.

5 On the Actions menu, click Void, and then click Yes to confirm the operation.

6 On the toolbar, click Save and Close to save the voided transaction record.

To record a check to be printed

1 On the Navigation pane, click Banking.

2 On the Banking home page, under Start a Task, click Write Checks.

3 On the Check form, under Bank account, keep Checking selected.

4 Fill in the information about the check.

5 Select the To Be Printed check box.

6 On the toolbar, click Save and Close.

216 **To record a deposit**

1   On the Navigation pane, click Banking.

2   On the Banking home page, under Start a Task, click Make Deposit.

3   In the Deposit form, in the Deposit in list, click Checking.

4   Under Payments Received, select the check boxes for customers from whom you received payments.

5   On the toolbar, click New Deposit Line.

6   Under Deposit Money from, click Vendor.

7   In the Name box, select the customer from whom you received a payment.

8   Fill in other details as required.

9   Click Record.

10 On the toolbar, click Save and Close.

219 **To record a credit card charge**

1   In the Navigation pane, click Banking.

2   On the Banking home page, under Start a Task, click Credit Card Charge.

3   From the Vendor Name list, select the name of the vendor.

4   In the Pay from list, select the credit card account.

5   In the Delivery Date field, enter the date when the purchase you are making needs to be delivered.

6   Fill in the details for the line item by entering a description (copier paper, for example), a quantity, and a unit price.

7   Click Save and Close.

221 **To reconcile a bank account**

1   On the Navigation pane, click Banking.

2   On the Banking home page, under Start a Task, click Reconcile Account.

3   In the Reconcile Account dialog box, in the Account list, select Checking.

4   In the Statement Date list, type the date of the statement you want to reconcile.

5   In the Ending balance box, enter the ending balance from the bank statement you are working from.

6   Click Next.

7   Select the check box for each transaction that matches a transaction on your bank statement.

8   Click Reconcile.

Chapter 14 Creating Reports to Manage Your Business

Page 231 **To display a report**

1   In the Navigation pane, click Reports.

2   On the Reports home page, in the Saved Reports pane, click the category that contains the report you want to view.

3   In the middle pane, click the report you want to view.

4   In the Select Date Range area, click the Range field's down arrow and then click the dates of the records you want to summarize.

5   Click Display.

232 **To print a report**

1   Display a report.

2   On the File menu, click Print.

3   Use the controls in the Print dialog box to set your print options and then click Print.

233 **To filter a report**

1   On the report window toolbar, click Filter Options.

2   In the Select Filter Option dialog box, click Balance.

3   In the Filter Options pane, select the desired comparison operator.

4   Type the value(s) to which you want to compare the report's contents.

5   Click Apply to apply the filter and leave the dialog box open, or click OK to apply the filter and close the dialog box.

Understand Microsoft Office
Small Business Accounting 2006,
page 1

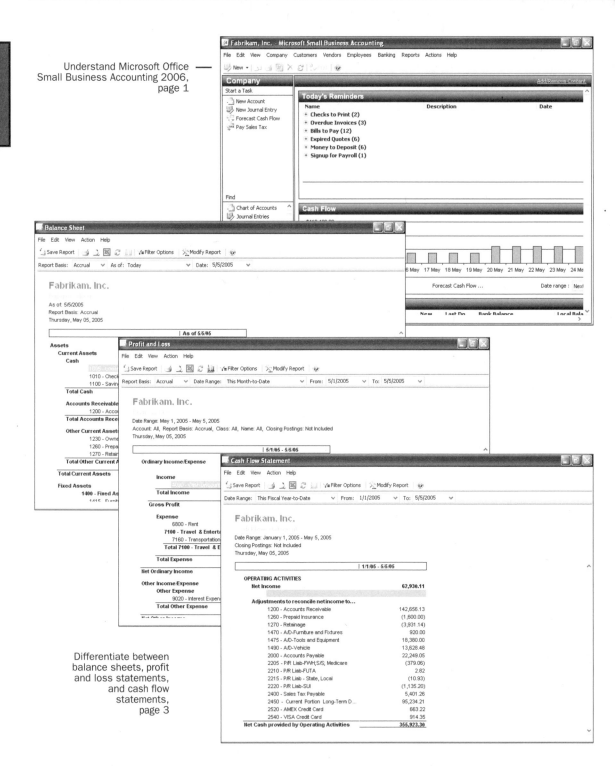

Differentiate between
balance sheets, profit
and loss statements,
and cash flow
statements,
page 3

Chapter 1 at a Glance

1 Getting to Know Microsoft Office Small Business Accounting 2006

In this chapter you will learn to:

✔ Define accounting as a practice.

✔ Use key accounting-related terms correctly.

✔ Fulfill your bookkeeping duties as a small business owner.

All businesses need to keep accurate records, but the complexity and sales volume of even the smallest companies outstrip the capabilities of paper- and spreadsheet-based record-keeping systems. Rather than try to bend generalized programs to your needs, you can turn to specialized software that is designed to handle your company's financial data.

Microsoft Office Small Business Accounting 2006 is a program that lets you record, analyze, and report on your company's income, assets, and expenses. For example, you can have Small Business Accounting list your total sales for a month, record the time individual employees spend on your company's projects, and find customers who are more than thirty days late in paying a bill. Small Business Accounting comes with a wide variety of reports you can use to summarize your company's operations. You can use those summaries to identify areas of interest and then drill down into the details to find areas where you can improve your company's operations.

In this chapter, you'll read about accounting as a process, learn key terms you'll encounter throughout this book and the general accounting literature, and find out how Small Business Accounting enables you to fulfill your record-keeping duties as a small business owner. The exercises in this book are based on data for two fictional companies, Fabrikam, a construction company, and Northwind Traders, a product-based sales company.

What Is Accounting?

The name of the program is Microsoft Office Small Business Accounting 2006, but what, specifically, is *accounting*? Accounting is the process of recording, classifying, summarizing, reporting, and assessing a company's business transactions. Recording transactions accurately enables you to analyze your company's performance, plan future endeavors, and fulfill your tax filing and payment obligations.

Warning   Do not wait until the end of a month or quarter to record your transactions! The longer you wait to record your credit card charges, payments received, and sales tax collected, the more likely it is that you'll forget something or make a mistake. Remember, you can easily waste your time trying to find misplaced information and, if you hire a tax professional to prepare your returns, you'll end up delaying your filing and paying your accountant for the time they spend looking for information they don't have.

Most accounting systems use *double-entry bookkeeping* to ensure that a corporation's books are correct. The basic assumption behind double-entry bookkeeping might be termed "conservation of money," which is another way of saying that if you write a company check for a $4,000 photocopier, you spend $4,000 from your checking account but gain $4,000 worth of office equipment. Similarly, if you build a computer for $500 and sell it for $795, you reduce your assets by $500 (the computer you no longer own), increase cash by $795, and generate $295 in profit.

Key Terms and Definitions

Every field uses its own specialized vocabulary to describe important concepts precisely. It might seem that accountants use terms such as *chart of accounts* and *balance sheet* to exclude you from their conversations, but in reality the accountants' goal is precision. Each specialized term denotes something important to their profession and, by extension, to your business. The following list highlights the most important terms you'll encounter when you use Small Business Accounting.

Note   You'll find a more complete glossary at the end of the book, but you'll see these terms used most throughout this book.

- **Account**   A record of financial transactions, usually grouped around a particular category that helps financial planners determine deductible expenses and taxable income. For example, you would track the cost of professional association memberships, journal subscriptions, and research materials in the *Dues, Publications, Books* account.

- **Accounting**   The process of recording, classifying, summarizing, reporting, and assessing a company's business transactions. The overall goal of accounting is to maintain a detailed and accurate picture of the company's performance and health.

- **Asset**   A resource that the corporation owns, such as cash, inventory, buildings, or equipment.

- **Balance sheet**   A financial statement that summarizes your company's status on a specific date.

- **Chart of accounts**   A list of your company's accounts and their balances.

- **Credit**   An entry on the right side of an account; debits are on the left. How a credit affects your bottom line depends on the type of account to which it is applied. A credit increases liabilities, equity, or income and decreases assets or expenses.

- **Debit**   An entry on the left side of an account; credits are on the right. How a debit affects your bottom line depends on the type of account to which it is applied. A debit increases assets or expenses and decreases liabilities, equity, or income.

- **Expense**   An amount spent on products or services related to your normal business operations, such as utilities or wages.

- **Income**   Revenue generated by selling products and services to your customers.

- **Liability**   A debt. Something owed, such as accounts payable or income taxes to be paid at a later date.

Your Accounting Duties as a Small Business Owner

Stated simply, your main accounting duty as a small business owner is to keep accurate records that enable you to operate your business effectively and file accurate tax reports. You should take the time to examine your income and expenses in detail, but you should also create reports that summarize your company's performance. The Securities and Exchange Commission (SEC) requires publicly traded companies to produce three reports: the *balance sheet*, the *profit and loss statement*, and the *cash flow statement*. Even if you haven't issued stock traded on any of the public markets, you can learn a lot about your business by examining these three reports. Small Business Accounting knows how to create these reports, and many others, by default.

The balance sheet reflects a company's financial position at a specific instant, such as at the end of a quarter or year. The balance sheet first lists the company's assets (such as office equipment, cash on hand, and goods), then lists the company's liabilities (such as taxes owed), and finally subtracts the liabilities from the assets to calculate the owner's equity in the corporation, as shown in a recent balance sheet for Fabrikam, our fictional construction company. Large loans, debt write-offs, and tax charges can affect how a company's balance sheet looks, but you can explain those elements in footnotes you attach to the balance sheet.

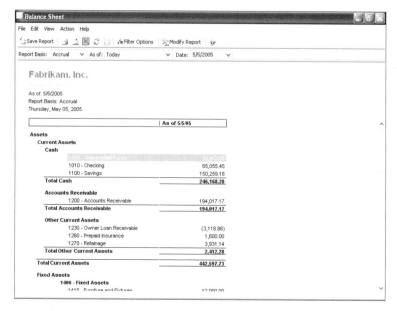

The second type of report you should create, the profit and loss statement (P&L), relates a company's performance over a period of time. Most companies release a P&L statement that covers their fiscal year, which often, but not always, corresponds to the calendar year of January 1 to December 31. The P&L statement starts with revenues and then details expenses, but it goes into more detail regarding expenses such as the cost of goods sold, operating expenses, taxes, loan interest, and other costs of doing business. Fabrikam's P&L statement covers only five days.

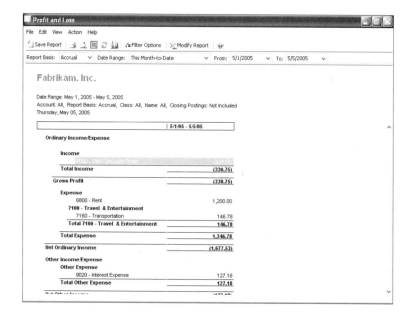

Note Author Curtis Frye started his small business' fiscal year on July 1, the date he founded the company.

The final basic report you should create, the cash flow statement, illustrates how your company manages the cash it generates through the sale of goods and services. Fabrikam's statement covers a four-month period. You must ensure that you have the cash available to pay the rent and power bill, repair or replace office equipment, and compensate employees. Examining the cash flow statement can reveal whether your spending patterns drain your company's cash reserves unnecessarily. If you do notice that your bank balances tend to run a bit on the low side, take a close look at how you spend your money and make changes as required.

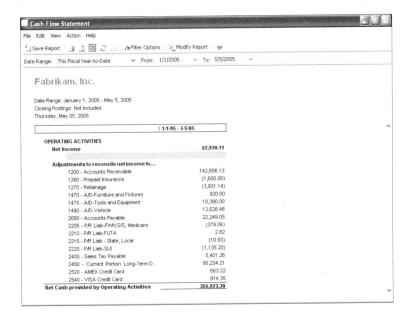

See Also For more information on your duties as a small business owner, download Internal Revenue Service Publication 583, "Starting a Business and Keeping Records," from *www.irs.gov/pub/irs-pdf/p583.pdf*.

Key Points

- Small Business Accounting enables you to record, analyze, and report on your company's income, assets, and expenses.

- You can learn a lot about your company from these three reports: the balance sheet, the profit and loss statement, and the cash flow statement.

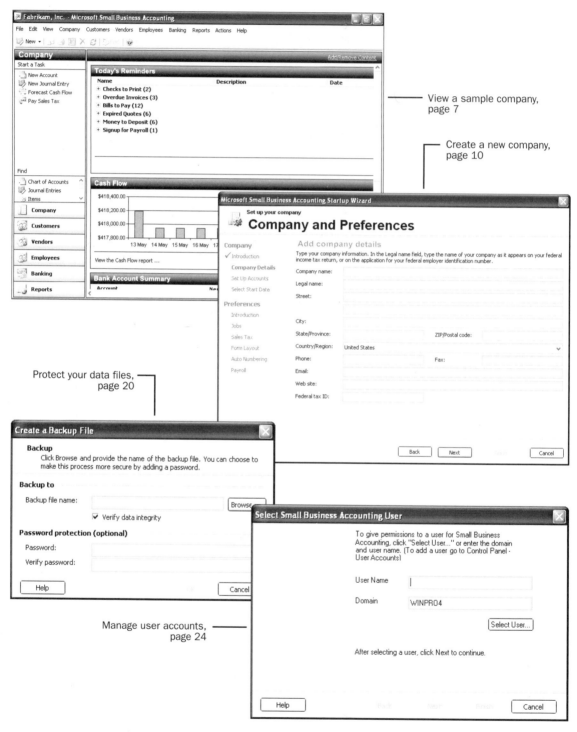

View a sample company,
page 7

Create a new company,
page 10

Protect your data files,
page 20

Manage user accounts,
page 24

Chapter 2 at a Glance

2 Setting Up a New Company

In this chapter you will learn to:

✔ View a sample company.

✔ Create a new company.

✔ Manage company data.

✔ Protect your data files.

✔ Manage user accounts.

Before you can begin entering your company's financial information into Microsoft Office Small Business Accounting 2006, you need to create a file to hold the data. In Small Business Accounting, you use the Startup Wizard to create a new company file that contains all of the tools you will need to manage your company's finances. After you create your company file, you can customize it, add user accounts to give your employees access to the data they need to do their jobs, and back up your files to prevent data loss that could cost you many thousands of dollars, and days or weeks of time, returning your company to order.

In this chapter you will learn how to view data from a sample company, create a new company, manage your company data, protect your data files, and manage users.

See Also   Do you need only a quick refresher on the topics in this chapter? See the Quick Reference entries on pages xiii–xvii.

Viewing a Sample Company

Microsoft Small Business Accounting organizes its data around a company, creating a set of accounts and reports you can use to manage inventory, track bank transactions, and create quotes. Company files can contain a lot of details that might seem overwhelming to a new user, but a quick look through one of the two sample company files that come with the program will build your familiarity with the program and show how it helps you manage your business.

In this exercise you will open a sample company file and view some of the reports, summaries, and projections you can create in Small Business Accounting.

BE SURE TO start Small Business Accounting before beginning this exercise.

1 In the **Start** dialog box, click **Open a Sample Company**.

2 In the **Select Sample Company** dialog box, select the **Service Based Sample Company** option.

3 Click **OK**.

The Fabrikam, Inc. sample data appears.

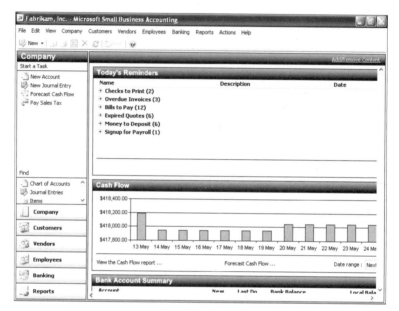

4 On the **Customers** menu, point to **Customer Lists**, and then click **Customers**.

A list of Fabrikam's customers appears.

5 On the **Company** menu, click **Company Home**.

The Fabrikam company home page appears.

6 Under **Cash Flow**, click the **Data Range** down arrow, and click **Next Month**.

The **Cash Flow** graph displays your cash flow for the next month.

7 On the **Vendors** menu, point to **Vendor Lists**, and then click **Purchase Orders**.

The list of open purchase orders appears.

8 Double-click purchase order number **1015**, from **Peoples' Plumbing, LLC**.

The purchase order appears.

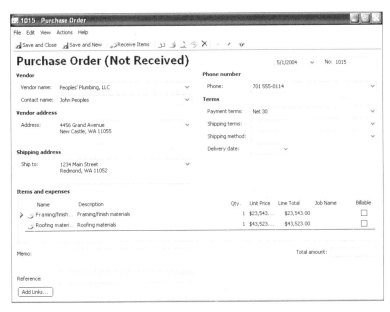

9 Click the **Close** box to close the purchase order.

10 On the **Company** menu, click **Company Home**.

The Fabrikam company home page appears.

11 On the **Reports** menu, point to **Vendors and Payables**, and click **A/P Aging Summary**.

The **A/P Aging Summary** report appears. This report lists invoices that have remained unpaid for 1 to 30 days, 31 to 60 days, and 61 to 90 days.

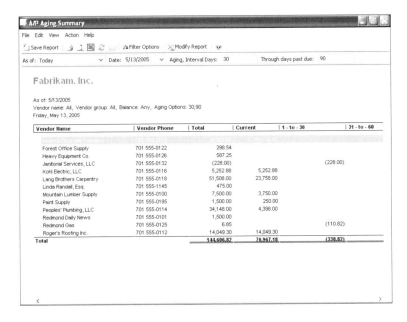

12 On the **File** menu, click **Close**.

The **A/P Aging Summary** report closes.

13 On the **File** menu, click **Close Company**.

The sample company file closes.

Creating a New Company

When you're ready to start tracking your company's information in Small Business Accounting, you can use the Startup Wizard to create the company's basic structure. After you have that structure in place, you can fill in details such as customers, products, and services.

Working Through the Startup Wizard

Setting up a new company in Small Business Accounting is a straightforward but somewhat lengthy affair. To make the setup process easier for you, Small Business Accounting helps you define your company by stepping you through the Startup Wizard.

In this exercise you will use the Startup Wizard to set up your company. All you need to do is answer questions about your company.

Important   The wizard asks you to collect your most recent checking, savings, credit card, and other bank statements; unreported and uncleared transactions; unpaid customer and vendor balances; and your company's assets, liabilities, and equity as of your company's start date. You must have this information on hand for your records to be accurate!

1   In the **Start** dialog box, click **Set Up Your Company** to launch the Startup Wizard.

2   Read the information on the **Company and Preferences** wizard page, gather the information the wizard recommends that you collect, and then click **Next** to display the **Company Details Introduction** wizard page.

3   Click **Next** to display the **Add Company Details** wizard page.

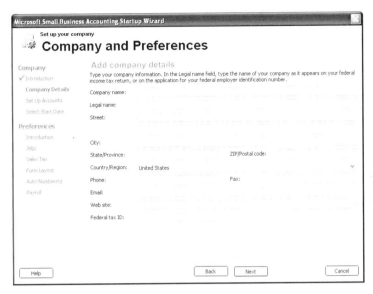

4   Type your company's information in the fields on the **Add Company Details** wizard page.

   Note   Your Federal Tax ID, also known as the Employer Identification Number (EIN), is the corporate equivalent of a Social Security Number. It is the number the Internal Revenue Service assigned to you after you filed Form SS-4, "Application for Employer Identification Number."

5   Click **Next** to display the **Set Up Accounts** wizard page.

6   Select the **Select Your Business Type and Have Small Business Accounting Suggest Accounts** option to have the program create standard accounts for your business.

7   Click **Next** to display the **Set Up Accounts (Cont.)** wizard page.

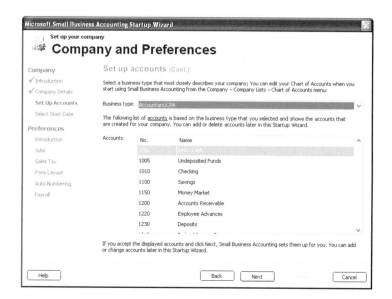

Note   Don't worry about getting the business type exactly right; you'll have the chance to add or remove accounts after you create your company.

8   Click the **Business Type** down arrow and select the business type that best describes your business.

9   Click **Next** to display the **Select a Fiscal Year and Start Date** wizard page.

10   In the **Beginning of the First Fiscal Year** field, type the first day of your company's first fiscal year.

11   In the **End of the First Fiscal Year** field, type the last day of your company's first fiscal year.

12   In the **Start Date** field, type the first day for which you will enter transactions.

Tip   You can click the down arrow at the right edge of any of the fields on the **Select a Fiscal Year and Start Date** wizard page to display a calendar control with which you can select a date.

13   Click **Next**, read the information on the **Preferences** introduction page, and then click **Next** again to display the **Select Jobs Preferences** wizard page.

14   Select the **Yes** option if you want to track jobs in Small Business Accounting, or select the **No** option if you don't want to track jobs.

Note   A job is a project performed on behalf of a client. If you run a metal fabrication business, a job might involve machining a custom part for a motorcycle builder.

15 Click **Next** to display the **Select Sales Tax Preferences** wizard page.

16 If your company collects sales tax, select the **Yes** option. If your company doesn't collect sales tax, or if you don't know your sales tax rates, select the **No** option.

If you selected **Yes** in the previous step, the wizard will ask if you collect sales tax at a single rate or at several rates. If you collect sales tax at several rates, you will need to enter the rates separately after you close the wizard. If you collect tax at a single rate and pay it to a single tax agency, the next wizard page will ask for information about the tax and the organization to which you pay it.

17 Click **Next**.

18 If you selected the **I Collect a Single Tax Rate and Pay It to a Single Tax Agency** option on the previous wizard page, the **Select Sales Tax Preferences (Cont.)** wizard page appears. In the fields provided, type in a name for the tax, the tax rate, and the name of the agency to which you pay the tax, and click **Next**

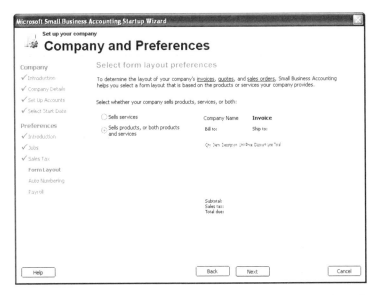

19 On the **Select Form Layout Preference** wizard page, select the **Sells Services** option if your company only sells services; otherwise, select the **Sells Products, or Both Products and Services** option.

20 Click **Next** to display the **Select Numbering Preferences** wizard page.

21 Select the check boxes next to the types of accounts to which you want Small Business Accounting to assign a unique identifying number.

Tip Assigning a unique identifying number to accounts, vendors, customers, etc. makes it easier to manipulate your Small Business Accounting data in database management systems such as Microsoft Office Access or Microsoft SQL Server. In general, it's a good idea to have Small Business Accounting assign a unique identifying number to items in every available category.

22 Click **Next** to display the **Set Up Payroll** wizard page.

23 If you plan to use the ADP Payroll for Small Business Accounting service, select the **Yes** option to have the program remind you to set up your payroll process after you close the wizard. If not, select the **No** option.

24 Click **Next**.

25 If you want to change any of your settings, click the **Back** button to revisit your selections. When you're done, click **Finish**.

The **Select Company File** dialog box appears.

26 In the **File Name** field, type your company's name and then click **Save**.

After you finish the first phase of the Startup Wizard, Small Business Accounting displays the **Small Business Accounting Startup Wizard Progress Checklist**.

Note If you'd like to take a break and resume setting up your company file later, click the **Close** button to close the wizard. You can restart the **Startup Wizard** at any time by opening the **File** menu and clicking **Startup Wizard**.

The **Small Business Accounting Startup Wizard Progress Checklist** provides a central location for you to add customers, vendors, products, and other corporate details. Because the tasks available in the **Small Business Accounting Startup Wizard Progress Checklist** duplicate tasks you might want to perform after you're done setting up your company, you can find the instructions on how to perform the tasks (creating a new account, editing customer information, and so on) in the chapters that cover those topics in more depth:

- For more information on adding and editing accounts, see Chapter 3, "Managing the Chart of Accounts and Journal Entries List."

- For more information on adding and editing customer information, see Chapter 5, "Setting Up Customer Information."

- For more information on adding and editing vendor information, see Chapter 11, "Purchasing from Vendors."

- For more information on adding and editing products and services, see Chapter 4, "Managing Products and Services."

Business Services Available to Small Business Accounting Users

The last item in the **Small Business Accounting Startup Wizard Progress Checklist** is **Business Services**, and it provides a link to a Web site with a list of services to which Small Business Accounting users can subscribe for additional fees. As of this writing, these services are listed:

- **ADP Payroll Services** handles the process of writing checks and submitting payroll tax payments.

- **Accept Credit Cards** provides a merchant account you can use to accept credit and debit card payments over the Web.

- **Buy Checks and Forms** offers pre-printed checks and business forms you can use to pay bills, send invoices, provide quotes, and so on.

- **Bank Online** enables you to download your banking transactions directly into Small Business Accounting.

- **Build a Web Site** provides a Web presence for business owners who have not created a Web site of their own.

- **Sell Online** provides an online shopping cart for visitors to a site.

- **Send Email Newsletters** enables you to keep your contacts informed of your company's activities, offers, and plans.

To close the **Startup Wizard**, click the **Close** button. You can re-start the **Startup Wizard** at any time by opening the **File** menu, and clicking **Startup Wizard**.

Changing Company Preferences

When you create a company, Small Business Accounting assumes that you want to do things a certain way. In many cases, Small Business Accounting remembers your choices from the Startup Wizard. For example, if you chose to assign unique identifying numbers to your accounts, that check box will be selected on the **Company** tab of the **Company Preferences** dialog box.

Most of the preferences you can set in the **Company Preferences** dialog box deal with how you handle customers, vendors, employees, and so on, so it wouldn't make much sense to go into a detailed discussion of the settings at this point. However, you will learn how to change the appropriate settings for each category in the chapters that cover those subjects later in the book.

In this exercise you will change your company preferences.

1 On the **Company** menu, click **Preferences**.

The **Company Preferences** dialog box appears.

2 Use the controls in the **Company Preferences** dialog box to set or change your company preferences.

3 Click **OK** to save your changes.

Managing Company Data

If you've been in business for a while, it's possible that you won't have to enter your company's data into Small Business Accounting directly. Instead, you might be able to import data from another Small Business Accounting company file or a file you maintained in another accounting program. You can also export data from a Small Business Accounting file to an *Extensible Markup Language (XML)* file, which you can then import into Small Business Accounting or another program that can handle XML data.

Importing Company Data from Small Business Accounting

If you have a company data file available in XML, you can import the data into Small Business Accounting by using the **Import Data** dialog box.

In this exercise you will import data from another Small Business Accounting file.

1   On the **File** menu, point to **Utilities,** and then click **Import.**

The **Import Data** dialog box appears.

2   Make sure **Microsoft Office Small Business Accounting Data** is selected, and click **OK.**

3   Click **Browse.**

The **Select a File to Import From** dialog box appears.

4   Navigate to the directory that contains the XML file you want to import, click the file name, and then click **Open.**

The **Select a File to Import** dialog box disappears.

5   Click **Import.**

A dialog box appears listing any records that were imported and any duplicates that were not.

6   Click **OK** to dismiss the dialog box.

Importing Company Data from QuickBooks

If you've previously used Intuit QuickBooks to handle your company's accounting, you'll find the transition to Small Business Accounting quick and painless. Small Business Accounting can import your data with just a few mouse clicks.

In this exercise you will use the Convert From QuickBooks Wizard to import company data from QuickBooks to Small Business Accounting.

1   In the **Start** dialog box, click **Import Data from QuickBooks.**

The Convert from QuickBooks Wizard appears.

2   Read the information on the **Introduction** wizard page and click **Next.**

3   Type your company's information into the fields on the **Company Contact Details** wizard page.

4 Click **Next** to display the **Select a Fiscal Year and Start Date** wizard page.

5 In the **Beginning of the First Fiscal Year** field, type the first day of your company's first fiscal year.

6 In the **End of the First Fiscal Year** field, type the last day of your company's first fiscal year.

7 In the **Start Date** field, type the first day for which you will enter transactions.

8 Click **Next** to pass the **Instructions for Migration** page.

9 Click **Next** to display the **Select QuickBooks Master Records** wizard page.

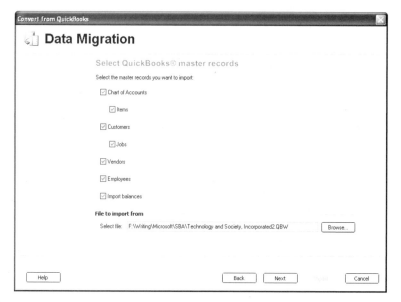

10 Clear the check box next to any data type you do not want to migrate to Small Business Accounting.

11 If the file you want to migrate doesn't appear in the **File to Import From** field, click the **Browse** button, use the **Select File** dialog box to locate the file you want to migrate, and click **Open**.

12 Click **Next**.

The program verifies that the file you identified contains valid data and can be migrated to Small Business Accounting.

13 Click **Import**.

The **Save Company** dialog box appears.

14 Use the controls in the **Save Company** dialog box to define a name and save location for your new corporate data file.

15 Click **Save**.

Small Business Accounting imports your data. When the import is complete, the program displays the **Import Completed** wizard page.

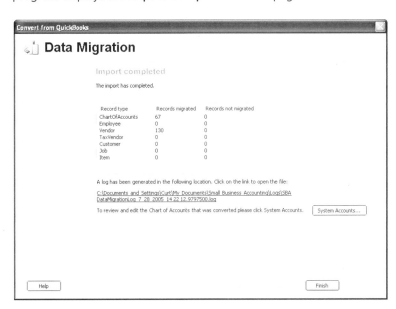

16 Click **Finish** to close the Convert from QuickBooks Wizard and display the company data you imported.

Exporting Company Data

If you work with an accountant, you should consider allowing the accountant to work on copies of your company data while you keep the original file on your computer. After your accountant verifies your data and generates your tax forms for the quarter or year, you can import the verified file back into Small Business Accounting and continue to record your company's transactions. In this exercise you will export company data from Small Business Accounting.

BE SURE TO open a sample company file before beginning this exercise.

1 On the **File** menu, point to **Utilities,** and then click **Export**.

The **Export Data** dialog box appears.

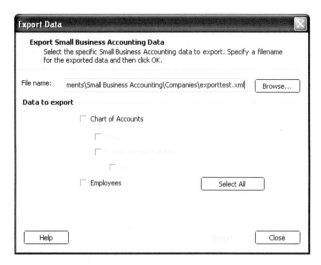

2 Click **Browse**.

The **Select a File to Export to** dialog box appears.

3 Either click a file to export data to an existing file or type a file name to export data to a new file.

4 Click **Save**.

The **Pick a File to Export to** dialog box disappears.

5 Under **Data to Export**, select the check boxes next to the data you want to export.

> **Tip** To export all of your data, click **Select All**.

6 Click **Export**.

Small Business Accounting exports your data to an XML file. A dialog box appears indicating the number of records exported successfully.

7 Click **OK** to dismiss the confirmation dialog box.

8 Click **Close** to dismiss the **Export Data** dialog box.

Protecting Your Data Files

Regardless of whether your company sells $10,000 or $10,000,000 in products and services in a year, you must make sure that nothing happens to your company's data! If you lose your records for a year, the absolute best thing that can happen is that you have to enter the data again. Yes, that's the best case. The worst-case scenario is that you can't find some of your records and you're unable to reconstruct what happened. You need to make several backup copies of your data, not just one!

Microsoft Office Small Business Accounting stores data in seven separate files. The following table summarizes those files' extensions and their roles in the program.

File Extension	Description
.sbd	A data file, stored by default in the SQL Server folder.
.sbc	A shortcut pointing to the location of the .sbd data file. The .sbc file is stored by default in the My Documents\Small Business Accounting\Companies folder of the administrator who set up your company in Small Business Accounting.
.sbl	An SQL log file, generated when you create a new company, import data from an XML file, or restore a backup file to a new company. The SQL log file is stored by default in the Program Files\Microsoft SQLServer\MSSQL$MICROSOFTSMLBIZ\Data directory.
.xml	An XML file, containing data exported from Small Business Accounting, stored by default in the My Documents\Small Business Accounting\Exported Data folder of the administrator who set up Small Business Accounting.
.log	A log file, generated when QuickBooks data are imported, a data file is repaired, your software is upgraded, and online banking or payroll processing is accessed by ADP. You must have selected the **Log Online Activities** check box in **Company Preferences** to create log entries. The log file is stored in the My Documents\Small Business Accounting\Logs directory of the administrator who installed Small Business Accounting.
.sbb	An uncompressed backup file, created when you upgrade your software or extracted when you open a compressed (.zip) file. The uncompressed backup file is stored in the My Documents\Small Business Accounting\Backups directory of the administrator who installed Small Business Accounting.
.zip	A compressed backup file, stored by default in the My Documents\Small Business Accounting\Backups folder of the administrator who set up Small Business Accounting.

Each file takes the name you assign to your backup copy. For example, the files for Fabrikam might have the names fabrikam.zip, fabrikam.sbc, fabrikam.sbb, and so on.

Creating a Backup File

You should back up your company files daily and write the files to a CD or DVD that you store somewhere outside your office. Too many backup copies have been lost to fires that both burned the computer that contained the original data and melted the backup CD. A bank safe deposit box is a great place to store your backup copies.

In this exercise you will create a backup copy of a company data file.

1   On the **File** menu, point to **Utilities**, and then click **Data Utilities**.

The **Small Business Accounting Data Tools** dialog box appears.

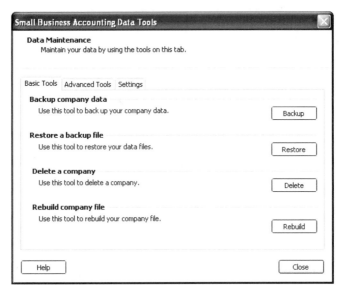

2   If necessary, click the **Basic Tools** tab.

3   Click **Backup**.

The **Create a Backup File** dialog box appears.

4   Click **Browse**.

The **Backup** dialog box appears.

5   Click the file you want to replace or type a name for the file in the **File Name** field.

6   Click **Save**.

The **Backup** dialog box disappears.

7   If desired, type a password for the file in the **Password** field and then type the same password in the **Verify Password** field.

8   Click **OK**.

Small Business Accounting creates a backup data file.

9   Click **OK** to dismiss the confirmation dialog box that appears.

10 Click **Close**.

The **Small Business Accounting Data Tools** dialog box disappears.

Restoring Data from a Backup File

If you need to restore your data from a backup file, you can do so quickly. In this exercise you will restore company data from a backup file.

1   On the **File** menu, point to **Utilities**, and then click **Data Utilities**.

The **Small Business Accounting Data Tools** dialog box appears.

2   If necessary, click the **Basic Tools** tab.

3   Click **Restore**.

The **Database Restore** dialog box appears.

23

4   Click the **Browse** button to the right of the **Backup Filename** field.

The **Restore** dialog box appears.

5   Click the file you want to restore and click **Open**.

The **Restore** dialog box disappears.

6   Click the **Browse** button to the right of the **Restore Backup File To** field.

The **Select Configuration File** dialog box appears.

7   Click the file you want to overwrite or type the name of a new file in the **File Name** field.

8   Click **Save**.

9   If the file is password protected, type its password in the **Password** field.

10 Click **OK**.

Small Business Accounting restores the file. The **Restore Complete** dialog box appears.

11 Click **OK** to dismiss the **Restore Complete** dialog box.

12 Click **Close**.

The **Small Business Accounting Data Tools** dialog box disappears.

Managing User Accounts

When you run a small business, you can be tempted to give all of your employees access to all of your office supplies, storage facilities, and computers. However, you should take care to limit what your employees can do when they view your company data in Small Business Accounting. Well-meaning employees can make mistakes with your data, but individuals with ill intentions can cause significant damage by altering or destroying data. It's best to allow individuals only the maximum permissions they require to do their jobs.

Small Business Accounting has five built-in user roles you can assign to your users. The table below summarizes the roles and what they can do.

Role	Description
Office Manager	Manages the day-to-day financial records of the company, including customer transactions, vendor transactions, banking transactions, and payroll. The Office Manager role has full access to most product areas but cannot set up the company, manage users, or restore or delete company data files.
Accountant	Responsible for reviewing, updating, and managing the financial data of the company. The Accountant role has all of the permissions of the Office Manager role and can set up online accounts and download transactions.
Owner	Limited access to all product features. An owner cannot create a new company, cannot install Small Business Accounting, and cannot manage user roles, unless he or she is an administrator on the computer running Small Business Accounting.
Sales Person	Responsible for handling customer transactions and most vendor transactions. The Salesperson role cannot carry out any banking, accounting (such as journal entries), or payroll transactions.
Read-Only User	Views customer and vendor transaction information but cannot add, delete, or update any information.

Creating a New Account

After you decide which role you want to assign to an employee, you can create an account for that person and assign privileges. The user accounts you create are based on Windows user accounts on your network, so you will need to know your employee's user name and the name of the computer on which that person has an account to give the individual access to Small Business Accounting.

In this exercise you will create a new user account.

1 On the **File** menu, click **Manage Users**.

The **Manage Users** dialog box appears.

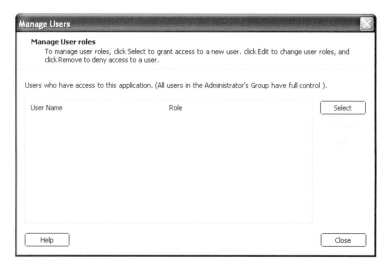

2   Click **Select**.

The **Select Small Business Accounting User** wizard appears.

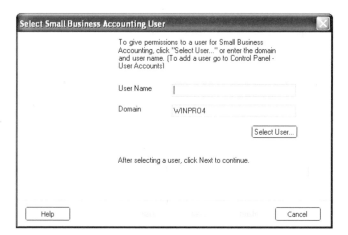

3   Click **Select User**.

The **Select User** dialog box appears.

4   In the **Enter the Object Name to Select** field, type the name of the user for whom you want to create a new account.

5   Click **Check Names**.

Small Business Accounting verifies that the Windows user name you type exists. If the user name doesn't exist, the program displays a message indicating it could not find the user name. Click **OK** to dismiss the information box, verify the user name, and re-type it in the **Enter the Object Name to Select** field.

6   Click **OK**.

The **Select User** dialog box disappears.

7   Click **Next**.

The next page of the **Select Small Business Accounting User** Wizard appears.

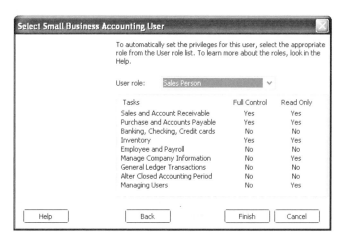

8   Click the **User Role** down arrow and select the role you want to assign to the selected user.

The permissions in the table below the **User Role** field change to reflect the selected role.

9   Click **Finish**.

Small Business Accounting creates the user role. The **Select Small Business Accounting User** Wizard disappears.

10   Click **Close**.

The **Manage Users** dialog box disappears.

Tip   You can change a user's role in the **Manage Users** dialog box by clicking the user name, clicking **Edit**, making changes in the **User Privileges** dialog box, and clicking **OK**.

Deleting an Account

If you have an employee who leaves the company or no longer requires any access to your Small Business Accounting data, you should delete that person's account immediately. Leaving unnecessary accounts on your system gives potential attackers many more ways to get into your books and do harm.

In this exercise you will delete a Small Business Accounting user account.

1 On the **File** menu, click **Manage Users**.

The **Manage Users** dialog box appears.

2 In the **Users Who Have Access to This Application** list, click the user account you want to delete.

3 Click **Remove**.

A verification dialog box appears.

4 Click **OK** to verify that you want to delete the account.

Small Business Accounting deletes the account.

5 Click **Close**.

The **Manage Users** dialog box disappears.

CLOSE Small Business Accounting.

Key Points

■ You should take the time to open a sample company file and familiarize yourself with the reports, windows, and options available to you in Small Business Accounting.

■ You can create a new company file by using the Startup Wizard. The wizard can take some time to complete, so don't hesitate to work on part of the process and return to it later.

■ Small Business Accounting users can transfer data from QuickBooks to by using the Convert from QuickBooks Wizard.

■ Make backup copies of your data to prevent catastrophic data loss.

■ Assign specific roles to each of your employees. Assigning roles limits how your employees can affect your company's data and limits the possibility for unintentional or intentional damage.

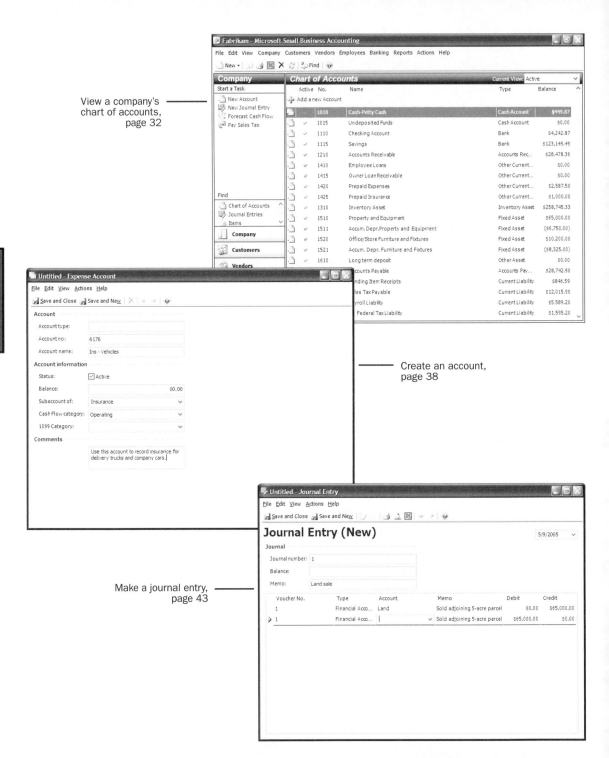

View a company's chart of accounts, page 32

Create an account, page 38

Make a journal entry, page 43

Chapter 3 at a Glance

3 Managing the Chart of Accounts and Journal Entries List

In this chapter you will learn to:

✔ View a company's chart of accounts.

✔ Modify the view of the chart of accounts.

✔ Create an account and edit account information.

✔ Merge accounts.

✔ Make a journal entry.

✔ View an account register.

✔ Edit or void a journal entry.

Accurate accounting requires attention to many details. The framework that supports detailed recordkeeping about each of a business's transactions, whether income or expense, *asset* or *liability*, is a *chart of accounts* that reflects the company's operations. Building a chart of accounts is one of the tasks you perform when you set up a company in Microsoft Office Small Business Accounting 2006. You can have Small Business Accounting create a basic chart of accounts designed for your type of business when you work through the Startup Wizard, and add accounts to the basic set later, or you can create a chart of accounts on your own.

In this chapter, you'll learn how to view the chart of accounts and create and edit accounts. You'll also learn how to work with journal entries. You use journal entries to record transactions such as the opening balance of an account, depreciation charges, the sale of an asset, or accounting adjustments.

See Also Do you need only a quick refresher on the topics in this chapter? See the Quick Reference entries on pages xvii–xx.

Viewing the Chart of Accounts

A company's chart of accounts lists the individual accounts that together show the company's financial picture. The chart of accounts is made up of different kinds of accounts: *balance sheet* accounts for assets and liabilities, income and expense accounts that reflect day-to-day activities of a business, and system accounts such as *accounts receivable*, *accounts payable*, or discounts.

Note Small Business Accounting creates required system accounts when you set up your company.

In this exercise, you will view the chart of accounts for a company and learn about the different types of accounts included in the chart.

BE SURE TO start Small Business Accounting if it is not already running.

OPEN the Fabrikam sample company file.

1 In the **Navigation** pane, click **Company** or **Banking**.

2 Under **Find**, click **Chart of Accounts**.

A chart of accounts you can scroll through appears.

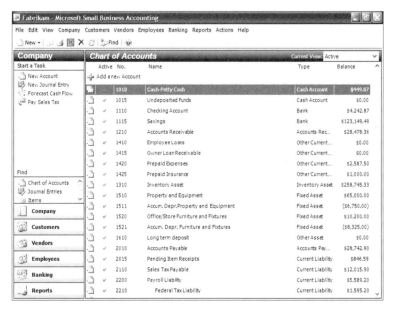

The chart of accounts lists asset accounts first, followed by liability accounts, equity accounts, and then income and expense accounts. If you have selected **Use Account Numbers** in **Company Preferences**, the account number determines the account's position within its grouping in the chart of accounts.

- **Asset accounts**   Asset accounts are numbered 1000 through 1999. These accounts include bank accounts, cash accounts (such as funds you haven't deposited or petty cash), inventory, and accounts receivable. Asset accounts also include a category called Other Current Assets, for items such as a short-term note receivable, a rent deposit, or another asset that you expect to convert to cash within one year. Fixed assets include land and other real estate, machinery, equipment, furniture, and fixtures. Fixed assets have a life greater than one year, and the cost of fixed assets is expensed over time through *depreciation*. Other assets might include a long-term note receivable or a certificate of deposit whose term exceeds 12 months.

  Note   The balance of an inventory asset account shows the value of the goods or supplies a company has on hand at a specific point in time. In Small Business Accounting, an inventory asset account summarizes all the inventory item records that are linked to the account. To set the opening balance for an inventory asset account, you need to create an inventory item and then enter the balance for that item. For more information about adding items to inventory, see Chapter 4, "Managing Products and Services."

- **Liability accounts**   Liability accounts are numbered 2000 through 2999. Liabilities include amounts payable to vendors and suppliers (the Accounts Payable account), loans you are paying back, tax liabilities, credit card purchases, and other debts. Liabilities such as sales tax and payroll taxes due, accrued salaries and wages, and short-term loans are considered current liabilities. Current liabilities are scheduled to be paid within one year. Long-term liabilities such as a mortgage are scheduled to be paid over a longer period of time.

- **Equity accounts**   Equity accounts are numbered in the 3000s. These accounts show a company's net worth, which is calculated by subtracting liabilities from assets. (In accounting, assets equal liabilities plus equity.)

- **Income and expense accounts**   Income and expense accounts are the accounts you work with most frequently from day to day. These accounts are included in an Income and Expense statement that shows business activity for a month, a quarter, or a fiscal year. Income accounts show revenue from sales of goods and services. A chart of accounts might also include an income account for the interest that an investment or a savings account earns. Expense accounts record amounts a company spends on insurance, phone, rent, and other products and services related to its operations. Interest payments are also recorded in an expense account. The account Cost of Goods Sold is the account that shows the cost of products and services that are entered into inventory and then sold.

■ **System accounts** System accounts (including the asset account named Accounts Receivable and the liability account named Accounts Payable) are set up by Small Business Accounting. You cannot delete a system account, but you can edit the account information. You can view a list of system accounts by choosing **Preferences** from the **Company** menu and then clicking the **System Accounts** tab.

See Also For more information about editing accounts, see "Adding and Editing Accounts" later in this chapter.

Tip You can use the lists on the **System Accounts** tab of the **Company Preferences** dialog box to select a different account to act as a system account. For example, for the system account Sales Tax Payable, you could use an account that you create named Sales Tax Due. If you have selected **Use Account Numbers** as a company preference and select a different account as a system account, the new account number will change the account's position within the chart of accounts.

■ **Opening Balances** Shows the account balance as of the start date for a company. This account should usually have a zero balance if assets equal liabilities plus equity.

■ **Accounts Receivable** Amounts that customers owe your company from the sales of goods and services are totaled in Accounts Receivable. You cannot post transactions directly to the Accounts Receivable account.

- **Accounts Payable**   Amounts your company owes to vendors and suppliers are reflected in Accounts Payable. You cannot post transactions directly to the Accounts Payable account.

- **Sales Tax Payable**   A current liability (due in less than one year). This account records the amount of sales taxes a company owes.

- **Cash Discount Given**   Records the amount of cash discounts (if any) you provide to customers based on terms of payment. (For example, some companies provide a discount if a customer pays a bill within 10 days or purchases a high volume of your goods or services.) The amount in this account offsets entries to your income account.

- **Cash Discount Taken**   Shows the amount of cash discounts you take on payments to vendors or suppliers when a discount applies. The amount offsets the expense account Cost of Goods Sold.

- **Undeposited Funds**   A cash account used to record amounts you've received but have not recorded in any other account.

- **Bank Charge**   An expense account used to record the amounts a company pays to its bank for charges such as account fees or transfer charges.

- **Retained Earnings**   An equity account that shows the balances from income and expense accounts at the end of a company's fiscal year. When a company's books are closed at the end of a fiscal year, balances from the income and expense accounts are moved to the Retained Earnings account.

- **Pending Item Receipts**   A current liability that reflects amounts a company owes for goods or services that the company has received but has not yet been billed for.

- **Write Off Account**   An account in which you record reductions to income for amounts that you deduct from the amounts owed to you. For example, you would use the Write Off Account to record the amount a customer's obligation is reduced as part of a payment plan.

Tip   You can print the chart of accounts by clicking **Chart of Accounts** in the **Navigation** pane, and then clicking **Print** on the toolbar.

Managing System Accounts After Migrating Data

When you migrate accounting records from a different accounting system (QuickBooks, for example) to Small Business Accounting, Small Business Accounting creates some basic required accounts, names the accounts, and designates these accounts as system accounts. When the company is created, Small Business Accounting also sets up accounts in the chart of accounts that correspond to system accounts. You can select other accounts in the chart of accounts to be system accounts.

To open the **Manage System Account**s dialog box, click **System Accounts** at the bottom of the **Import Completed** page in the Data Migration Wizard. For the account you want to change, select another account from the list as the system account. If you want to create a new financial account, select **Add a New Financial Account**.

Changing Your View of the Chart of Accounts

When you display the chart of accounts, it shows only active accounts and provides account information in five columns:

- ■   **Active**   A check mark in this column indicates that an account is active. The account is inactive if no check mark appears in this column.

- ■   **No.**   The account number. This column is visible if you chose to use account numbers in the settings for company preferences.

- ■   **Name**   The account's name.

- ■   **Type**   The type of account, such as Fixed Asset, Current Liability, Income, or Expense.

- ■   **Balance**   The current balance of the account.

Tip   To display up-to-date information in the chart of accounts, click the **Refresh** button on the toolbar.

You cannot sort the chart of accounts to change the order in which accounts are listed. However, you can add, remove, and change the layout of the columns. You can also filter the list of accounts to display either active or inactive accounts or all accounts.

In this exercise, you will change which columns are displayed in the chart of accounts and filter the account list.

OPEN the Fabrikam sample file if you have closed it.

1 In the **Navigation** pane, click **Company**.

2 Under **Find**, click **Chart of Accounts**.

3 On the **View** menu, click **Add/Remove Content**.

4 In the **Grid Customization** dialog box, click a column heading you want to add in the **Available Column Headings** list, and then click **Add**.

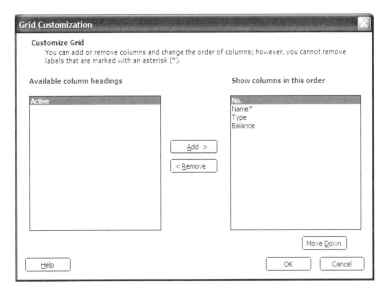

5 To change the order in which the columns appear, click the column you want to move in the **Show Columns in This Order** list, and then click the **Move Up** or **Move Down** button.

6 To remove a column from the chart of accounts, click the column heading in the **Show Columns in This Order** list, and then click **Remove**.

7 To filter the account list, open the **Current View** list at the top right of the chart of accounts, and then click **Active**, **Inactive**, or **All**.

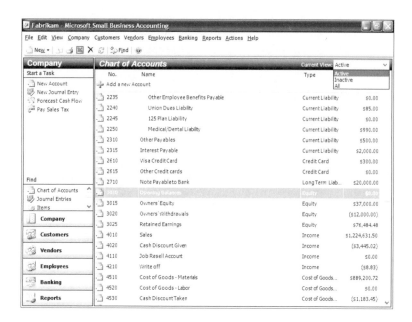

Adding and Editing Accounts

You can add accounts for assets, liabilities, income, and expenses to the basic chart of accounts that is created when you set up a company with the Small Business Accounting Startup Wizard. You can also build a chart of accounts from scratch if you did not select a standard chart of accounts in the Startup Wizard. When you create an account, you provide an account name and number and an opening balance. For credit card accounts, you also enter information such as the credit limit, bank name, and the last four digits of the card number.

When you add an account, you have the option of designating it a subaccount. A subaccount must be the same type of account as its parent account. For example, under an expense account named Advertising and Promotion, you could create a subaccount for expenses related to ads you place in printed material and a subaccount for ads you place on Web sites. By using subaccounts, you keep entries for related items under a single account.

In this exercise, you'll add an expense account to the chart of accounts for Fabrikam and then edit information for a different account. The account you add will be a subaccount of the Insurance account and will be used to record expenses for vehicle insurance.

OPEN the Fabrikam sample file if you have closed it.

1   In the **Navigation** pane, click **Company**.

2   Under **Start a Task**, click **New Account**.

3   In the **Select Account Type** dialog box, select the type of account you want to add, and then click **OK**. For this exercise, click **Expense**, and click **OK**. The title bar of the account form that opens shows the type of account you select.

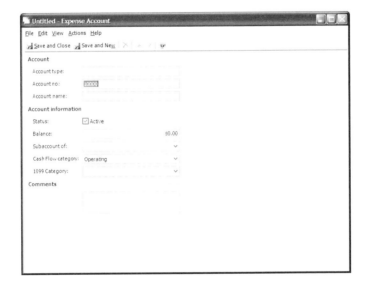

Important   You cannot change the type of account after you add an account.

4 In the account form, type 6176 in the **Account no.** box.

The **Account no.** box is displayed if you have **Use Account Numbers** selected as a company preference. You must include an account number if you are using them. Be sure to use a number related to the type of account so that the new account fits the organization of the chart of account and accounts of the same type are listed together. You can change an account number later if necessary by editing the account.

5 In the **Account name** box, type Ins – Vehicles. When creating an account, be sure to provide a descriptive name.

6 Keep the **Balance** box set to **$0.00**. The opening balance will often be zero for a new account, or it could reflect past transactions.

Note You can enter a balance for a new account only within the fiscal year in which you set up a company in Small Business Accounting. After the first fiscal year, the balance field is read-only. You will need to enter an opening balance through a journal entry. For more information about making journal entries, see "Making a Journal Entry" later in this chapter.

7 In the **Subaccount of** list, select Insurance.

8 In the **Cash Flow Category** list, keep **Operating** selected.

You can select Operating, Investing, or Financing in the **Cash Flow Category** list. The selection you make specifies how the account will appear on cash flow statements, which summarizes transactions in these three categories of your business activities.

Tip If you are uncertain about which cash flow category to use, open an account from the chart of accounts that is the same type and check how that account is categorized.

9 In the **1099 Category** list, make no selection for this account.

The **1099 Category** list reflects categories on 1099-MISC tax forms that you send to vendors who are 1099 vendors. The categories listed in Small Business Accounting relate to forms in the tax year 2004. You should check whether these categories have changed for the next year. If the categories have changed, you need to edit the category list in the **Modify 1099 Categories** dialog box. You can then edit the chart of accounts for the changes.

10 In the **Comments** box, type Use this account to record insurance for delivery trucks and company cars. Use the **Comments** box to provide information about how to use an account.

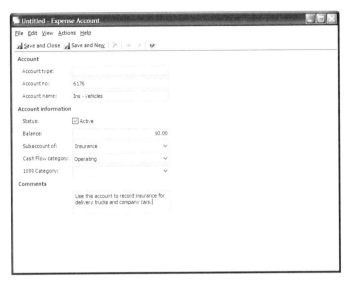

11   Click **Save and Close** to finish creating the account. (If you are adding a series of accounts, click **Save and New**.)

12   In the chart of accounts, select the account **Prepaid Expenses** (no. 1810), which is an asset account.

13   On the **Actions** menu, click **Edit Account**. (You can also right-click the account name and then click **Open Selected Items**.)

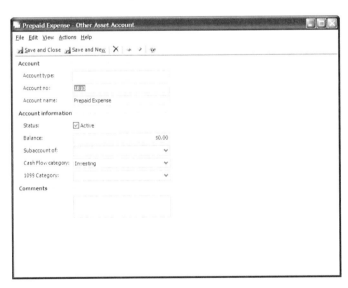

14   Under **Account Information**, clear the **Status: Active** check box.

15   In the **Comments** box, type No prepaid expenses for this company at this time.

16   On the toolbar, click **Save and Close**.

> **Tip**   As the number of accounts in the chart of accounts grows, you can use the **Find** tool to quickly locate an account. With the chart of accounts displayed, click **Find** on the toolbar. In the **Look for** box, type a keyword related to the account. In the **Search under** box, select the heading for the column you want to search. Click **Find**. The chart of accounts now shows only the accounts that meet the criteria you provided. To show the full chart of accounts again, click **Clear**.

Direct and Indirect Costs

Many businesses have direct costs such as labor, materials, and shipping. These expenses fluctuate depending on the volume of business activity. Businesses also have expenses such as rent and utilities that are not tied directly to the volume of products or services they sell. These costs remain fairly static. One reason to separate direct expenses from indirect expenses is to calculate your overhead (your indirect expenses), which can be a factor in how you determine the price at which you sell your goods and services. When you review your chart of accounts, any cost that's related to manufacturing a product or to the actual service you provide should be considered a direct expense.

Merging Accounts

After working with transactions in your chart of accounts for a period of time, you might see that similar information is recorded in two accounts. To get a better perspective on the activity in these accounts, you would like to see the information combined when you view financial statements. By using the **Merge Financial Accounts** dialog box, you can merge two accounts. After you merge two accounts, you cannot separate them again. Also, the accounts you merge must be the same type of account. (For example, you cannot merge an income account with an expense account.) You cannot merge bank and credit card accounts.

In this exercise, you'll merge two accounts from the Fabrikam chart of accounts.

OPEN the Fabrikam sample file if you have closed it.

1   On the **Company** menu, point to **Merge Accounts**, and then click **Merge Financial Accounts**.

The **Merge Financial Accounts** dialog box appears.

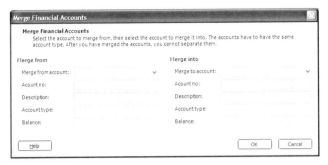

2   Under **Merge From**, in the **Merge from Account** list, click the account you want to merge from. The account number (if you are using account numbers), description, type, and balance are displayed and cannot be edited.

3   Under **Merge Into**, in the **Merge to Account** list, click the account into which you will incorporate the records.

Small Business Accounting combines the two accounts into a single account.

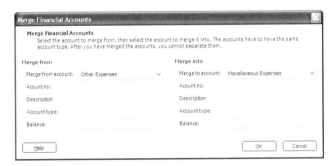

4   Click **OK**.

Making a Journal Entry

Journal entries record business transactions. While recording all your business transactions through journal entries is possible, you usually make a journal entry for a transaction that is not part of the day-to-day operations of your company. With a journal entry, for example, you can enter the opening balance for an account, record depreciation charges, record the sale of assets, or adjust entries that need a correction. You will record the majority of transactions when you create invoices, pay bills, or perform similar operations.

With each journal entry, you record activity in at least two different accounts. You debit one account by entering a positive amount, and you credit a second account by entering a negative amount. How the debit and credit entries affect your bottom line depends on the type of account the entries are applied to. A debit increases an asset or expense account and decreases a liability, equity, or income account. A credit increases a liability, equity, or income account and decreases an asset or expense account.

See Also For more information on double-entry bookkeeping, see "What Is Accounting" in Chapter 1, "Getting to Know Microsoft Office Small Business Accounting 2006."

Note After you add a transaction, you cannot delete it. If an entry is incorrect or invalid, you can edit the entry or mark it void.

In this exercise, you will open a journal entry form and make a journal entry.

OPEN the Fabrikam sample file if you have closed it.

1 In the **Navigation** pane, click **Company**.

2 Under **Start a Task**, click **New Journal Entry**.

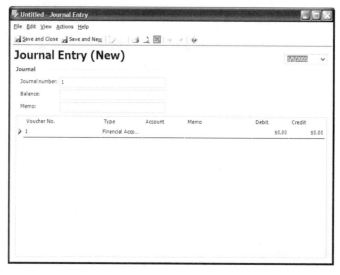

By default, the date shown is the current date. You can change the journal entry date by typing a date or by clicking the arrow to open the calendar and then selecting a date.

The journal number is filled in by Small Business Accounting. The number is incremented from the previous number recorded in this field. It is good practice not to change this number. The total of the debits and credits you enter in a journal entry is calculated in the **Balance** box. You cannot post the journal entry if the balance is not zero.

3 In the **Memo** box, type Sale of asset. You should use the **Memo** box to describe the purpose of the journal entry.

4   In the **Voucher No.** box, keep the number **1**.

You use the voucher number to identify the entry. (The voucher number is not the same as the journal number.) Small Business Accounting displays the same number on the next row when you go to that row. Small Business Accounting changes the voucher number when a journal entry is in balance.

Tip   If you are simply adjusting financial accounts, you can record multiple transactions (which have different voucher numbers) in a single journal entry. However, you should change the number when you start a new entry so that each entry can be easily identified.

5   In the **Type** column, select **Financial Account**. The selection you make from this list specifies which accounts are displayed in the **Account** column.

- **Financial Account**   The Account list shows all financial accounts from the chart of accounts. Select Financial Account for transactions such as adjusting bookkeeping errors or sales of assets.

- **Vendor**   The Account list shows the list of vendors you've set up in Small Business Accounting. Select Vendor to make changes for transactions related to discounts or payments, for example, or to correct an error. A debit reduces a vendor payable, and a credit increases a vendor payable. You can make only one vendor entry for each journal entry. The balancing account line must be an entry for a financial account. For more information about creating and working with vendors, see Chapter 11, "Purchasing from Vendors."

- **Customer**   The Account list includes the list of customers you've set up in Small Business Accounting. Use Customer to modify receivable balances for discounts or payments or to correct errors. As with a vendor entry, the balancing account line must be an entry for a financial account, and you can make only one customer entry for a journal entry. For more information about creating and working with customers, see Chapter 5, "Setting Up Customer Information."

- **Tax Code**   The Account list shows all tax agencies. Use this option to make adjustments to sales tax balances due as a result of discounts, payments, or errors. The balancing line must be a Financial Account.

6   In the **Account** column, click **Land** (account number 1410).

Tip   You can add a new account while making journal entries by clicking **Add a New Account** at the top of the **Account** list.

7   In the **Memo** box, type additional information about each entry. For this example, type **Sold adjoining 5-acre parcel.**

> **Note** Entering a memo is not required, but it is helpful when reviewing your financial records to have a brief description of specific journal entries.

8 In the **Credit** column, type 65000. Remember that a credit entry decreases the amount of an asset account.

9 Press [Tab] until you create a new entry row in the journal.

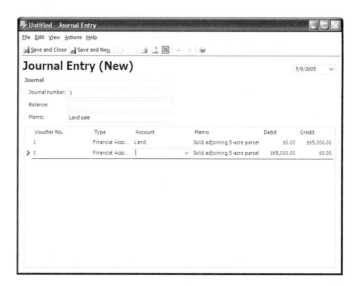

Small Business Accounting creates the balancing entry for you, adding a debit in the same amount as the credit entry made in step 8. Notice also that the **Balance** box shows **$0.00**, meaning that the debit and credit are equal.

10 In the **Account** list in the second row, select **Savings**.

11 In the **Memo** column, changing the memo to read *Deposit from land sale*.

12 On the toolbar, click **Save and Close**. (To save the entry and make another, click **Save and New**.)

> **Note** Additional columns appear on the journal entry form if you select specific company preferences. For example, if you select **Use Class** on the **Company** tab of the **Company Preferences** dialog box, the journal entry form includes the **Class** column (as do other forms related to income and expense records). Classes let you classify income and expenses in categories such as sales region. The **Job Name** column appears in the journal entry form if you have selected **Use Job** to track

expenses by job. If you select **Use Job**, a journal entry form also includes a **Billable** column. Select the check box in this column to indicate that an expense can be billed to a customer.

Viewing an Account Register

Each transaction for an account is displayed in the account register. The account register shows the date and number for each journal entry, a memo that describes the entry, the other account or accounts affected by the transaction, the amount of the reduction or increase, and the account balance. With the account register for an account open, you can also make a new journal entry related to the account.

In this exercise, you'll view the account register for an account and change the appearance of the account register.

OPEN the Fabrikam sample file if you have closed it.

1 In the **Navigation** pane, click **Company**.

2 Under **Find**, click **Chart of Accounts**.

3 In the chart of accounts, double-click the **Undeposited Funds** account.

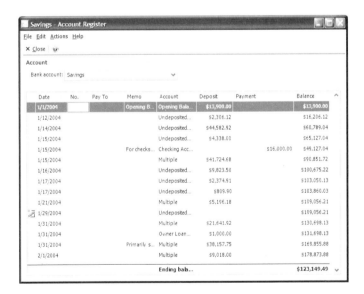

4   To initiate a journal entry from the account register, click **Add new Journal Entry** at the bottom left corner of the **Account Register** window.

5   To edit information for the account, click **Open Accounts Details** on the **Actions** menu.

6   To sort the list of transactions in ascending or descending order, click a column title. The arrow beside the column name indicates the sort order.

         Note   If you sort the account register by a column other than the **Date** column, the amounts shown in the **Balance** column change, but the ending balance does not.

7   To change the width of a column, drag the column divider beside the column heading.

8   To change the order of the columns, select a column heading and drag it to the location where you want the column to appear.

9   To close the account register, click **Close** on the toolbar.

Transaction Reports

The **Actions** menu in the account register form includes commands for viewing the Transaction History report and the Transaction Journal report. The Transaction History report displays transaction dates, types, amounts, status, and related information. You can modify the Transaction History report to see information about who created a transaction and when information was modified.

The Transaction Journal report includes accounting entries over a period of time. The report is arranged by types of entries (customer payments, journal entries, and vendor bills, for example). Each entry shows the debits and credits that make up the transaction. The Transaction Journal report often provides useful context when you are reviewing and reconciling financial statements.

Using Credit Card Account Registers

When you view the register for a credit card account, the information includes the account creation date, document numbers, names, charges, and balances. To use the account register to enter details about credit card charges, click **New Transaction** on the **Actions** menu. You then use the dialog box that appears to indicate whether the credit card transaction is a charge, a credit, or a fee. For more information about working with credit card transactions, see Chapter 13, "Managing Bank Accounts and Transactions."

Editing and Voiding Journal Entries

After you have made a journal entry, you cannot delete the entry. If you could delete a journal entry, the transaction history of your company would be vulnerable to tampering and your financial records too easily put out of balance.

You can, however, *void* a journal entry if the entry is no longer applicable. Also, you can make adjustments to the details of a transaction by editing a journal entry.

Deleting Accounts and Changing Account Status

If you are no longer using an account, you can delete the account or mark it inactive. However, you can delete an account only if it's not a system account and if you have not recorded an opening balance or any transactions associated with the account. You can change the status of a system account or an account for which you've recorded transactions to *inactive*. To make an account inactive, select the account name in the chart of accounts, and then click **Make Inactive** on the **Edit** menu. When you make an account's status inactive, you cannot select the account from lists in dialog boxes and forms, for example, because the account will not appear in those lists. To post an entry to an inactive account, you need to display inactive accounts in the chart of accounts (by selecting **Inactive** or **All** in the **Current View** list) and then select the account you need to work with.

In this exercise, you will edit a journal entry and mark a journal entry void.

OPEN the Fabrikam sample file if you have closed it.

1 In the **Navigation** pane, click **Company**.

2 Under **Find**, click **Journal Entries**.

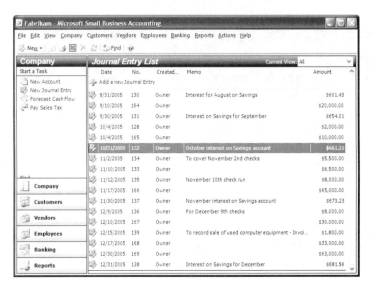

3   Double-click the journal entry you want to edit.

4   On the toolbar, click **Edit**.

5   Change the information on the journal entry form.

6   On the toolbar, click **Save and Close**. To save your changes and create another journal entry, click **Save and New**.

7   In the list of journal entries, double-click the journal entry that you need to void.

8   On the **Actions** menu, click **Void**.

9   To confirm that you want to void the entry, click **Yes**.

10 Click **Save and Close**.

CLOSE the Fabrikam sample file.

Tip You can filter the list of journal entries by clicking **Voided**, **Nonvoided**, or **All** in the **Current View** list. You can change the order of the columns in the list of journal entries, or add or remove columns from the list, by clicking **Add/Remove Content** on the **View** menu.

Tip If Microsoft Office Excel is installed on the computer on which you are running Small Business Accounting, you can export the list of journal entries to Excel. In the **Navigation** pane, click **Company**, and then click **Journal Entries** under **Find**. On the toolbar, click **Export to Excel**. Save the file in Excel if you want to refer to it again for analysis.

Key Points

- The chart of accounts represents the categories of a business's operations.
- You can select a default set of accounts when you set up Small Business Accounting. Later, you can add accounts and edit account information.
- The journal is the history of each transaction you record. For each journal entry, the amount of the debits and credits must be equal.
- You cannot delete a journal entry. You can, however, edit a journal entry to correct the entry or mark a journal entry void.

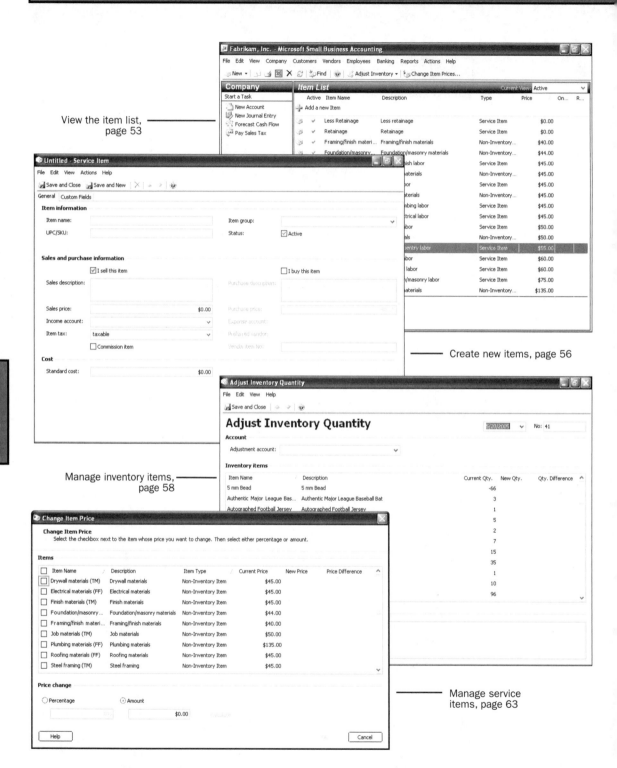

View the item list,
page 53

Create new items, page 56

Manage inventory items,
page 58

Manage service
items, page 63

Chapter 4 at a Glance

4 Managing Products and Services

In this chapter you will learn to:

✔ View the item list.

✔ Create new items.

✔ Manage inventory items.

✔ Manage service items.

✔ Manage custom item groups.

Your business makes money by selling two things: what you have and what you know. Microsoft Office Small Business Accounting classifies a product or service you have for sale as an *item*; the program maintains a master list of all of your items, whether they are currently for sale or not, and enables you to modify their entries as needed to reflect price changes, inventory results, and other factors.

In this chapter you will learn how to view the item list; use available item types; create and edit items; and change item prices, quantities, and values.

See Also   Do you need only a quick refresher on the topics in this chapter? See the Quick Reference entries on pages xx–xxiii.

Viewing the Item List

Every business, whether a consultancy or a manufacturer, makes money by selling products and services. Small Business Accounting represents the things you sell, such as an hour of consulting or a steel ball bearing, as an item. To display all of the items your company sells, on the **Company** menu, point to **Company Lists**, and click **Items** to display the **Item List**.

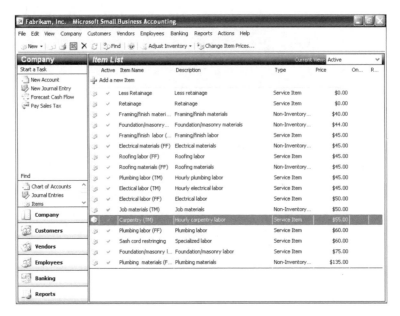

The **Item List** contains an entry for each item your company sells, although it can also display items that are not currently available for sale. Items that are available for sale are called *active items*, and they have a check mark in the **Active** column. Items that are not available for sale are *inactive items*. By default, the **Item List** displays only active items, but you can display both active and inactive items by clicking the **Current View** down arrow and clicking **All**.

At the top of each column is a header that describes the data stored in the column. You can sort the contents of the **Item List** alphabetically based on a column's contents by clicking the column's header. For example, clicking the **Item Name** header in the Fabrikam sample file's item list would result in the **Item List** arrangement sorted alphabetically by item name.

Clicking a column header once sorts the **Item List** in ascending order based on the column's value; clicking the column header again sorts the **Item List** in descending order.

If your business sells many different items, they might not all fit on one screen. Small Business Accounting enables you to limit the items that appear in the **Item List** by creating a filter. To create a filter, open the **Actions** menu and click **Find**, which displays the **Find** toolbar.

Tip If you prefer to use keyboard shortcuts, you can press Ctrl+F to display the **Find** toolbar.

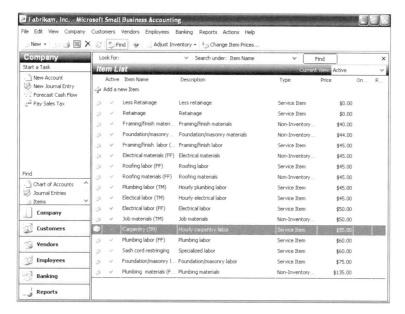

After you display the **Find** toolbar, type the terms you want to find into the **Look for** field, select the column in which you want to find the terms by using the **Search under** down arrow, and then click **Find**. To remove the filter, click **Clear**. When you're done using the **Find** toolbar, open the **Actions** menu and click **Find** (or press Ctrl+F) to dismiss the toolbar.

In this exercise, you will view, filter, and sort the **Item List**.

OPEN the Fabrikam sample file if you have closed it.

1 On the **Company** menu, point to **Company Lists**, and click **Items**.

The **Item List** appears.

2 Click the **Current View** down arrow, and then click **Inactive**.

Small Business Accounting displays items Fabrikam no longer offers for sale.

3 Click the **Current View** down arrow, and then click **Active**.

Small Business Accounting displays items Fabrikam offers for sale.

4 Click the **Type** column header.

Small Business Accounting sorts the **Item List** by item type.

5 Click the **Item Name** column header.

Small Business Accounting sorts the **Item List** by item name.

6 On the **Actions** menu, click **Find**.

The **Find** toolbar appears.

7 In the **Look for** field, type framing.

8 Verify that **Item Name** appears in the **Search under** field.

9 Click **Find**.

The **Item List** displays **Framing/Finish Labor (FF)** and **Framing/Finish Materials (FF)**, the two items that contain the word *framing* in their **Item Description** field.

10 Click **Clear**.

The filter deactivates, and the **Item List** displays all of Fabrikam's items.

11 On the **Find** toolbar, click the **Close** button.

12 The **Find** toolbar disappears.

Creating New Items

Some businesses can thrive without offering more than a core set of products and services, but the vast majority of companies need to update their offerings to retain current customers and attract new ones. Whenever your company offers a new product or service for sale, you create a new item in your company file.

When you want to add a new item, open the **New** menu, and choose **New Item** to display the **Select Item Type** dialog box. You can then choose from four different item types:

- **Service** includes labor or consulting provided to the customer.

- **Inventory** includes items your company keeps in stock.

- **Non-Inventory Item** includes items your company needs to order before you can provide them to your customers.

- **Kit** is a collection of items sold as a group.

Selecting **Service**, **Inventory**, or **Non-Inventory Item** displays a form you can use to fill in details about the item, such as its name, price, and description. However, if you select the **Kit** option, Small Business Accounting displays a form for creating a kit.

Clicking in the first **Item Name** field in the list near the bottom of the form displays a down arrow. When you click the down arrow, Small Business Accounting displays a list of your company's active items. Click the item you want to add and fill in the rest of the fields to add the first item to your kit. You can then click in the second and subsequent **Item Name** fields to add items to the kit.

When you select **Service**, **Inventory**, or **Non-Inventory Item**, you can use the same form to enter items you purchase from vendors as well as items you sell. Small Business Accounting distinguishes between the two types of items and allows you to designate an item as both types.

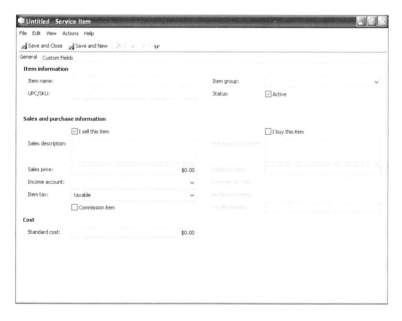

In the form for the new item, you can select the **I Sell This Item** check box to indicate that you provide the product to your customers. If you select the **I Buy This Item** check box, you indicate that you purchase the product or service from a vendor. And, yes, you can select both check boxes. If you purchase building supplies for use on your projects and to sell in your showroom, you would select both the **I Buy This Item** and the **I Sell This Item** check boxes and fill in the item's information in both areas.

If you find that you want to add information about an item that doesn't fit in the standard form fields, you can create a custom field to hold that information. To create a custom field for an item, display the item, click the **Custom Fields** tab, and then click the **Customize** button at the lower left corner of the item window to display the **Customize Form** dialog box.

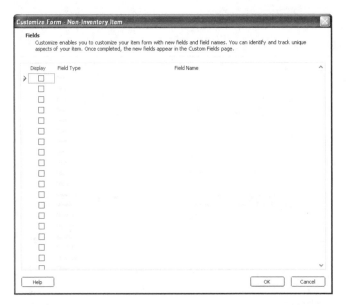

In the **Customize Form** dialog box, select the check box next to the type of field you want to create (text, date, number, or check box), type a name for the field in the **Field Name** column, and then click **OK**.

Managing Inventory Items

If your company sells items in a store or on the Web, you need a way to track items you keep in inventory. The process you follow to create a new inventory item requires you to enter the number of items you have in stock, the quantity at which you should re-order the item, and the item's value. After you create an inventory item, you can change its value and change the number you have in stock to reflect broken or misplaced units.

Creating a New Inventory Item

The first step in managing inventory items is to add the items to your **Item List**. In this exercise you will create a new inventory item.

1   In the **Start** dialog box, click **Open a Sample Company**.

The **Select Sample Company** dialog box appears.

2   Select the **Product Based Sample Company** option.

3   Click **OK**.

The Northwind Traders company file appears.

4   On the toolbar, click the **New** button down arrow, and then click **New Item**.

The **Select Item Type** dialog box appears.

5   Select the **Inventory** option.

6   Click **OK**.

The **Untitled - Inventory** form appears.

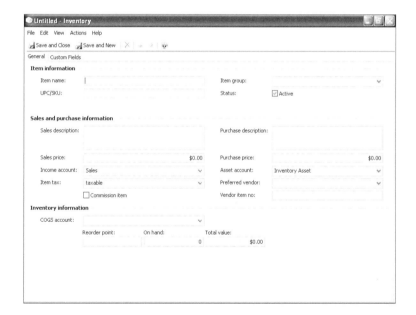

Note   The name of the form that appears depends on the type of item you're creating.

7 In the **Item Name** field, type Baseball Display Box.

8 Click the **Item Group** down arrow, and then click **Baseball Gear**.

9 In the **Sales Description** field, type Baseball display box for windows.

10 In the **Sales Price** field, type 10.

11 Click the **Income Account** down arrow, and then click **Sales**.

12 In the **Purchase Price** field, type 5.

13 Click the **Asset Account** down arrow, and then click **Inventory Asset**.

14 In the **Reorder Point** field under **Inventory Information**, type 15.

15 In the **On Hand** field, type 45, and press ⌷Enter⌷.

   $225.00 appears in the **Total Value** field.

16 Click the **Custom Fields** tab.

   The **Custom Fields** tab page appears.

17 Click **Customize**.

   The **Customize Form – Inventory** form appears.

18 Select the check box in the **Display** column next to the first row that contains **Date** in the **Field Type** column.

19 Press the ⌷Tab⌷ key.

   The insertion point appears in the **Field Name** field.

20 Type Re-evaluation Date and click **OK**.

The new field appears on the **Custom Fields** tab page.

21 Click **Save and Close**.

Small Business Accounting saves your item and closes the item form.

Changing Quantity On Hand

Despite everyone's best efforts to make sure that no items are misplaced or broken, the quantity of an item you have in your physical inventory might be different from the number of those items you purchased. Whether the items go missing without a good explanation or have to be written off after someone drops a crystal figurine on a concrete floor, you will need to adjust the quantity of those items in your company file.

In this exercise you will change the quantity of an item you have on hand.

OPEN the Northwind Traders sample file if you have closed it.

1 On the **Vendors** menu, point to **Adjust Inventory,** and then click **Adjust Quantity**.

The **Adjust Inventory Quantity** form appears.

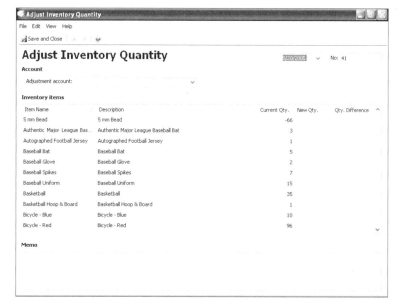

2 Click the **Adjustment Account** down arrow, and then click **Advertising Expenses**.

3 On the **Basketball** row of the **Inventory Items** list, click in the **Qty. Difference** field.

4 Type -5 and press [Tab].

The value **30** appears in the **New Qty.** field, and Small Business Accounting highlights the next row in the **Inventory Items** list.

5 Click **Save and Close**.

The **Adjust Inventory Quantity** form disappears.

Changing Quantity and Value

Prices change all the time due to inflation, resource scarcity, responses to competitor pricing, and the perceived value of collectible goods. For example, Fabrikam might use a certain type of steel support in their construction projects and bill customers for those materials. If your supplier charges more for those supports, you will need to pass that increase on to your customers. You can change the quantity and value of inventory items from within the **Item List** by clicking **Adjust Inventory**, clicking **Adjust Quantity and Value**, and then using the controls in the **Adjust Inventory Quantity and Value** form to enter the new data.

If you need to change an item's inventory level but don't have the **Item List** open, you can point to **Adjust Inventory** on the **Vendors** menu, and then click **Adjust Quantity and Value** to open the same form.

In this exercise you will change the quantity and value of an inventory item.

OPEN the Northwind Traders sample file if you have closed it.

1 On the **Vendors** menu, point to **Adjust Inventory,** and then click **Adjust Quantity and Value**.

The **Adjust Inventory Quantity and Value** form appears.

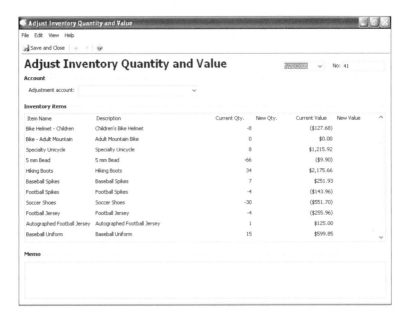

2   Click the **Adjustment Account** down arrow, and then click **Cost of Goods – Materials**.

3   In the **Inventory Items** list, on the row of the **Autographed Football Jersey**, click in the **New Quantity** field.

4   Type 3.

5   On the same row, click in the **Current Value** field.

6   Type 250 and press Tab.

7   Click **Save and Close**.

Managing Service Items

Unlike inventory items, which are physical objects you can count, service items are intangible goods such as labor or intellectual property. When you sell the only auto-graphed football jersey you have in stock, you can't sell another copy. By contrast, if you and your employees know how to frame a house, you don't lose that ability when you sell your service to a client.

If you sell electronic goods, such as software programs made available for download and electronic books published in Microsoft Reader or another format, you should list those items as service items. Because you can make perfect copies of the items, you don't keep them in inventory and won't run out of those items regardless of how many you sell.

Creating a service item is similar to creating an inventory item, but you don't need to define the quantity of that item you have in stock or set a re-order level. In this exercise you will create a new service item.

1   If necessary, on the **File** menu, click **Close Company** to close any open company files.

2   In the **Start** dialog box, click **Open a Sample Company**.

The **Select Sample Company** dialog box appears.

3   Select the **Service Based Sample Company** option.

4   Click **OK**.

The Fabrikam company file appears.

5   On the toolbar, click the **New** button down arrow, and then click **New Item**.

The **Select Item Type** dialog box appears.

6   Select the **Service** option.

7   Click **OK**.

8   The **Untitled – Service** Item form appears.

9 In the **Item Name** field, type Sash cord restringing.

10 Click the **Item Group** down arrow, and then click **Time & Materials**.

11 In the **Sales Description** field, type Sash cord restringing for windows.

12 In the **Sales Price** field, type 60.

13 Click the **Income Account** down arrow, and then click **Framing/Finish Services**.

14 In the **Standard Cost** field, type 60.

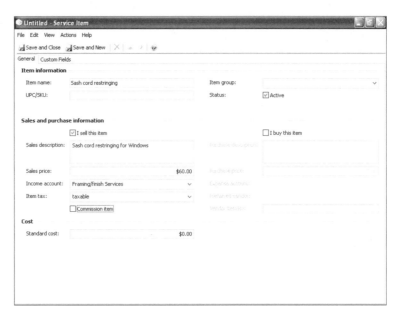

15 Click **Save and Close**.

16 Small Business Accounting saves your new service item.

The **Untitled – Service Item** form disappears.

Changing Service Item Prices

Item prices can change quickly, whether due to inflation, increased wholesale prices, or decreased raw materials cost. You can change the price of any item by editing the item in the **Item List**. In this exercise you will change the prices of items you offer for sale.

OPEN the Fabrikam sample file if you have closed it.

1 On the **Vendors** menu, click **Change Item Prices**.

The **Change Item Price** form appears.

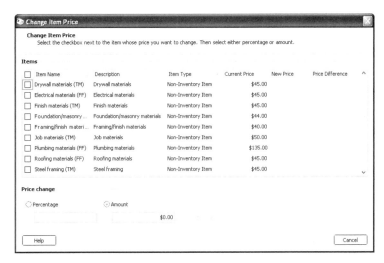

2 Select the check boxes next to **Plumbing Labor (FF)** and **Plumbing Labor (TM)**.

3 Under **Price Change**, select the **Percentage** option.

4 In the **Percentage** field, type 5.

5 Click **Calculate**.

On the **Plumbing Labor (FF)** row, **$63** appears in the **New Price** column and **$3** appears in the **Price Difference** column. On the **Plumbing Labor (TM)** row, **$47.25** appears in the **New Price** column and **$2.25** appears in the **Price Difference** column.

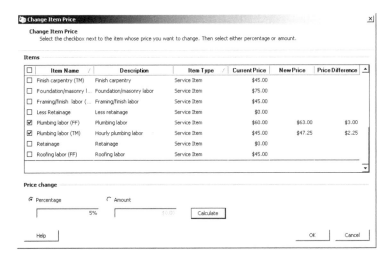

6 Click **OK**.

Small Business Accounting saves your new prices and closes the form.

Changing the Status of an Item

When you own a small business, you must be sensitive to the wants and needs of your customers. One outcome of your analysis might be to discontinue certain products or to no longer offer unpopular services. For example, if you sell one hour of drywall installation a month, you should probably stop offering the service and train the technicians to perform another task. You might also be faced with the unfortunate circumstance of having a vendor go out of business, leaving you unable to offer one of their products for sale. Of course, if you find another source for the product, you can start selling it again.

Items you have for sale are active items; items you no longer sell are inactive items. In this exercise you will change an item's status.

OPEN the Fabrikam sample file if you have closed it.

1 On the **Company** menu, point to **Company Lists**, and then click **Items**.

The **Item List** appears.

2 Click the **Current View** down arrow, and then click **Inactive**.

The inactive items appear in the **Item List**.

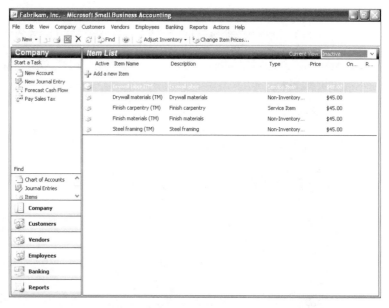

3 Right-click the **Drywall Labor (TM)** list item and then click **Make Active**.

The **Drywall Labor (TM)** item disappears from the list of inactive inventory items.

4   Click the **Current View** down arrow, and then click **Active**.

The list of active inventory items appears.

5   Right-click the **Drywall Labor (TM)** list item, and then click **Make Inactive**.

The **Drywall Labor (TM)** item disappears from the list of active inventory items.

Deleting an Item

If you entered an item incorrectly, you should either edit it or, if the item's information is completely wrong, delete it from your company file entirely. You can only delete an item from your company file if you have never had any units of the item in stock and have never sold a unit of that item. Otherwise, you need to mark the item as inactive to ensure that you don't offer it for sale.

In this exercise you will delete an item.

OPEN the Fabrikam sample file if you have closed it.

1   On the **Company** menu, point to **Company Lists**, and then click **Items**.

The **Item List** appears.

2   Click the **Sash Cord Restringing** item.

3   On the toolbar, click the **Delete** button.

A verification dialog box appears.

4   Click **Yes**.

Small Business Accounting deletes the item from the **Item List**.

Managing Custom Item Groups

One of the more attractive tasks you can accomplish in Small Business Accounting is creating custom reports to display an overview of your business. For example, you can determine how much of your revenue comes from hourly labor, how much of your costs come from buying lumber, and what types of consulting result in the best return. When you create a report though, Small Business Accounting will list the items in alphabetical order without regard to which items are related to one another. However, if you assign the items to groups such as hourly labor, consulting, and product sales, you can sort the report by group to provide a much clearer picture of how much each of your business elements contributes to your company's performance.

Note   You assign an item to a group when you create or edit the item, but you can edit that selection at any time.

In this exercise you will create and edit a custom group.

OPEN the Fabrikam sample file if you have closed it.

1 On the **Company** menu, point to **Manage Support Lists,** and then click **Item Group List**.

The **Modify Item Groups** dialog box appears.

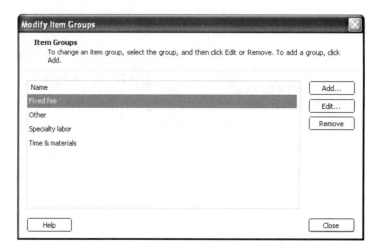

2 Click **Add**.

The **Add or Edit Item Group Name** dialog box appears.

3 In the **Item Group Name** form, type Contract Labor.

4 Click **OK**.

The new **Contract Labor** group appears in the **Modify Item Groups** dialog box.

5 If necessary, click **Contract Labor**.

6 Click **Edit**.

The **Add or Edit Item Group Name** dialog box appears.

7 In the **Item Group Name** dialog box, type Specialty Labor.

8 Click **OK**.

The group name changes to **Specialty Labor**.

9 Click **Close**.

The **Modify Item Groups** dialog box disappears.

See Also For more information on creating reports based on item groups, see "Creating Custom Reports" on page 235.

Avoiding Negative Inventory

One of the problems faced by businesses of all sizes, but particularly by small businesses, is keeping popular products in stock. It can be tempting to take all of your customers' orders without regard to whether you have the stock on hand to fill the order, but you should look very carefully at your sales orders to ensure there are no items on back order. You should also communicate very clearly to your customers that they will not receive their entire order at one time, and give them the option to change their order.

You can also have Small Business Accounting warn you whenever you create an order that would require more units of a product than you have in stock (that is, create a negative inventory level). To have Small Business Accounting warn you whenever an order would result in negative inventory, open the **Company** menu, click **Preferences**, click the **Vendors** tab of the **Company Preferences** dialog box, select the **Check for Item Quantity On Hand** check box, and then click **OK**.

Key Points

- You can find all of your items on the item list, which you can search and sort to make it easier to manage your items.

- If your company offers a new product or service for sale, you can add a new item to the item list.

- Manage your inventory items in the item list by ensuring that you haven't passed your re-order level.

- Service items are always in stock, but make sure your billing rates reflect your costs and the competition's prices.

- Creating custom item groups helps you track how specific types of products (for example, luxury items such as hot tubs or saunas) contribute to company revenue.

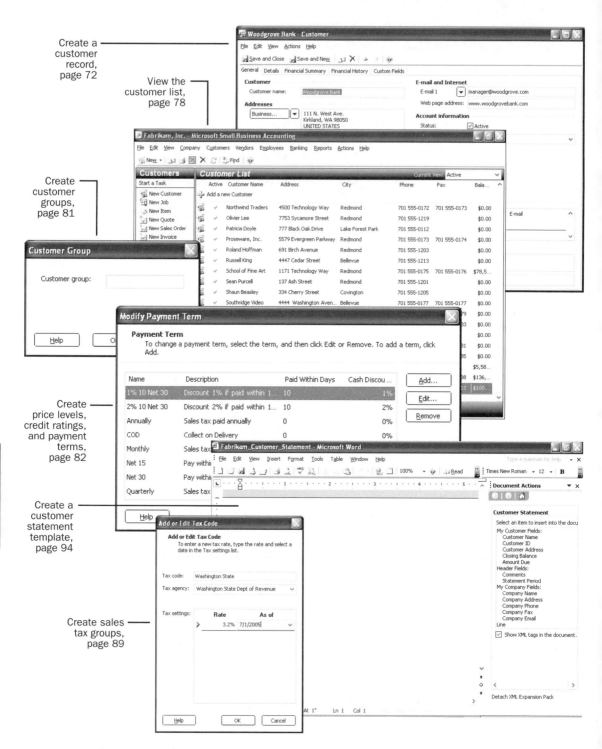

Create a
customer
record,
page 72

View the
customer list,
page 78

Create
customer
groups,
page 81

Create
price levels,
credit ratings,
and payment
terms,
page 82

Create a
customer
statement
template,
page 94

Create sales
tax groups,
page 89

Chapter 5 at a Glance

5 Setting Up Customer Information

In this chapter you will learn to:

✔ Create a customer record.

✔ View the customer list.

✔ Create customer groups.

✔ Create price levels, credit ratings, and payment terms.

✔ Set up sales tax agencies and sales tax codes.

✔ Create sales tax groups.

✔ Add details to a customer record.

✔ Create a customer statement template.

Much of the work involved in operating a small business is related to managing customers. Two key elements of a detailed and informative accounting system are the facts and the figures it stores about a business's customers, including up-to-date contact information and a history of financial transactions. You work with customer records to maintain an accurate list of contact information. Documents such as invoices, quotes, and payments make up the breadth and depth of a customer's financial history.

In addition to maintaining customer contact information such as names, addresses, and phone numbers, you need information about the details required to administer a customer's account. For example, you need to know if a discount is applied to the orders a customer makes, and you need to specify a customer's credit rating and tax status, and the payment terms by which a customer is expected to pay.

In Microsoft Office Small Business Accounting 2006, you initiate your work with customer information at the **Customers** home page. The home page provides links to your customer list and to tasks such as creating a customer record, preparing an estimate, issuing an invoice, and viewing reports that summarize information about customer payments.

In this chapter, you will be introduced to the **Customers** home page and learn how to create and work with customer data in Small Business Accounting. You'll learn how to create a customer record, how to view and sort the customer list, and how to define the discounts, payment terms, pricing levels, and the tax group that you apply to a customer account. You'll also learn how to design and modify a template in Microsoft Office Word that you can use to provide account statements to your customers.

71

See Also Do you need only a quick refresher on the topics in this chapter? See the Quick Reference entries on pages xxiii–xxvi.

Creating a Customer Record

Customer records in Small Business Accounting are used to store basic contact information such as a customer's name, street and e-mail addresses, phone numbers, and Web site. After you've built a history with a customer, customer records also provide a quick view of a customer's financial picture—information such as the current balance, year-to-date sales, payment history, and a transaction summary.

Entering Basic Customer Information

The **Customers** home page is a centralized workspace from which you can manage customer information, initiate documents such as quotes and invoices, process payments, view customer reports, and find links to articles and other information that can help you manage your small business.

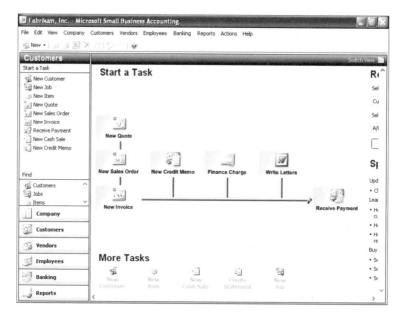

Note The **Spotlight** section on the **Customers** home page includes links to information related to small business services, accounting, and customers. Many of the links take you to Web pages that are part of the Microsoft Small Business Center (*www.microsoft.com/smallbusiness*). The links in the **Spotlight** section are updated regularly.

Tip   You can view the **Customers** home page in the task flow view or in list view. To change the view, click **Switch View** in the upper right corner of the home page.

From the **Customers** home page, you can access customer records. Each customer record displays one address, phone number, and fax number at a time; however, you can put in several different entries for each field. For example, in addition to a business phone number, you can enter numbers for a mobile phone and home phone, the phone number for a customer's assistant, and another phone number of your choice.

You can enter up to three fax numbers—business, home, and other. To select which address, phone number, or fax number you want to enter, click the down arrow next to the field.

Linking to Existing Files

In some cases, you might have had contact with a customer before you entered that customer's information into a customer record. For example, a customer might have sent you an e-mail message that you saved as a Word file. If you'd like to link to those documents, click **Add Links** on the customer record form to display the **Select File To Link To** dialog box.

In the **Select File To Link To** dialog box, select a document or documents related to this customer that you have stored on your computer. You can link more than one document to the customer's record, which means that by using the **Add Links** button, you can build the customer's record over time so that it provides a location from which you can easily access a wide range of documents and information related to the customer.

Customizing the Customer Record Form

You can use the **Customize Form** dialog box to define additional fields on the customer record in which to store customer information. You can create text, date, number, and check box fields. For example, you can add a check box to indicate whether a customer is a preferred customer—one that you want to include when you advertise promotions. You can create a number field in which to store the number of employees a customer has and a text field in which to store additional comments about a customer.

Important The custom fields you create appear on the customer record form for every customer. The custom fields are not unique to a specific customer.

Viewing a Customer's Financial History

As you enter and process transactions for a customer, the fields on the **Financial History** and **Financial Summary** tabs on the customer record form are filled in. You can then use the customer record to gain quick access to financial information about a customer. The **Financial History** tab displays customer payments, invoices, and quotes. To open a specific item listed on the **Financial History** tab, double-click the item. The **Financial Summary** tab displays information such as whether the customer has payments that are past due, their total outstanding balance, and their purchases for the current month, the current year, the last year, and over the customer's lifetime.

See Also For more information about working with payments, see Chapter 10, "Handling Customer Payments." For more information about invoices, see Chapter 9, "Preparing and Managing Invoices." For more information about quotes, see Chapter 7, "Generating and Managing Quotes."

In this exercise, you will create a customer record. The exercise focuses on entering contact information for a customer. You'll also see what kind of financial information you can view in a customer record and learn how to create a custom field that you can use to add to the information you store on the customer record form. In exercises later in the chapter, you'll learn how to create customer account tools such as price levels, discounts, and customer groups and how to add these details to a customer record.

OPEN the Fabrikam sample company file.

1   On the **Navigation** pane, click **Customers**.

The **Customers** home page appears.

2   Under **More Tasks**, click **New Customer**.

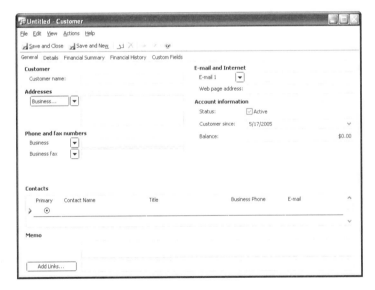

The customer record form appears. This form contains five tabs that you use to enter and view information. When you create a customer record, you work mainly on the **General** tab and the **Details** tab.

3   In the **Customer Name** box, type Kim Ralls.

4   Click the **Addresses** down arrow and then click **Business**.

The **Address** dialog box opens.

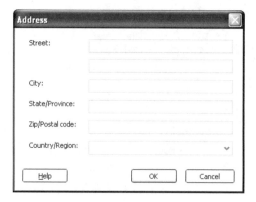

5 In the appropriate fields of the **Address** dialog box, type P.O. Box 1001, Redmond, WA, 22841.

Note Many small businesses will have customers in only one country or region. If your customer base includes customers from more than one country or region of the world, in the **Address** dialog box, click the **Country/Region** down arrow, and then click **Add a New Country/Region** to build the list of locations. In addition to the name of the country or region, you can enter a country code that is based on standards set by the International Organization for Standardization (ISO). You can find the list of ISO codes at *www.iso.org*

6 Click the **Addresses** down arrow, click **Ship To**, and then type 456 Water St., Redmond, WA 22841.

7 Under **Phone and Fax Numbers**, in the **Business** field, type (425) 555-0101.

8 In the **Business Fax** field, type (425) 555-0102.

9 In the **Account Information** area, keep the **Active** check box selected.

10 In the **Customer Since** field, change the date to 6/12/2005.

11 Make sure the entry in the **Balance** field is $0.00.

Note After you save a customer record in which you've entered an opening balance, the **Balance** box is no longer displayed on the customer record form. The balance information appears in the **Balance Due** area of the **Financial Summary** tab.

12 Under **Contacts**, click in the **Contact Name** field and type Gabriele Cannata, press [Tab] twice, and then type (425) 555-0101 in the **Business Phone** field.

Note You can enter more than one contact, but only one contact can be selected as the primary contact.

13 On the customer record form, click the **Custom Fields** tab.

14 On the **Custom Fields** tab, click **Customize**.

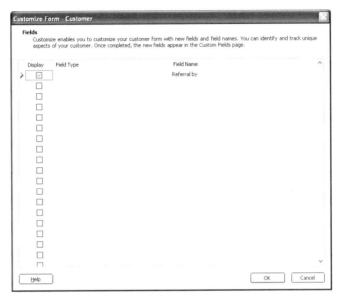

15 In the **Customize Form - Customer** dialog box, select the check box for the first entry for a **Number** field. In the **Field Name** column, type No. of Employees, and then click **OK**.

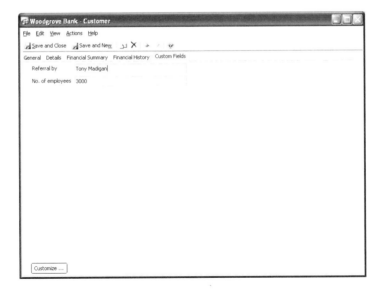

16 Click **Save and Close**.

The customer record form disappears.

Viewing the Customer List

The customer list in Small Business Accounting displays key customer contact information and the amount of the customer's balance. You can use the customer list as the departure point for working on the information about a particular customer in more detail. For example, you can update contact information, add contact details, view financial status, and enter account details such as credit limits or similar information. You can also sort the customer list to group customers. For example, you can group customers by city or sort the customer list to see customer balances in ascending or descending order.

Tip   By default, the customer list displays only active customers. You can display all customers or only inactive customers by using the **Current View** list at the upper right corner of the customer list.

By default, customers are listed in alphabetical order by customer name. You can click a column heading to sort the list by different criteria. Sorting by city, for example, lets you group customers into geographic areas. By clicking the column heading **Balance**, you can see which customers owe you the most money and which customers owe you the least.

You can delete a customer record if you have not recorded any transactions for that customer and the customer has no financial history. If you have recorded transactions for a customer record, you can mark the customer record inactive but you cannot delete it. A customer record that is marked inactive is not displayed in customer lists in dialog boxes or forms. To delete a customer record from the customer list, right-click the customer in the list and then click **Delete**.

To make a customer record inactive, right-click the customer record in the customer list and then click **Make Inactive**. You can change an inactive customer's status back to active by selecting the customer record in the customer list and then clicking **Make Active** on the **Edit** menu.

In this exercise, you'll learn how to view and sort the customer list in Small Business Accounting and how to organize the columns of information that the customer list displays.

OPEN the Fabrikam sample file if you have closed it.

1   On the **Navigation** pane, click **Customers**.

The **Customers** home page appears.

2   In the **Find** area of the **Customers** home page, click **Customers**.

The **Customer List** appears.

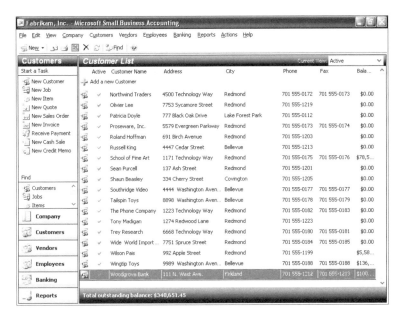

3 At the top of the **Customer List**, click the column heading **City**.

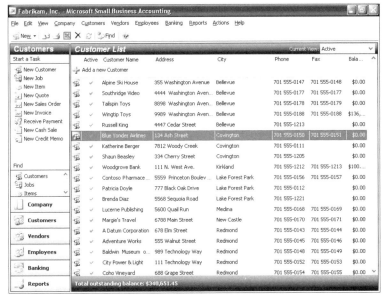

4 On the toolbar, click **Find**.

5 In the **Look for** box, type Bellevue.

6 In the **Search under** list, choose **City**.

7 Click **Find**.

The **Customer List** now shows only the customers that match the criteria you used.

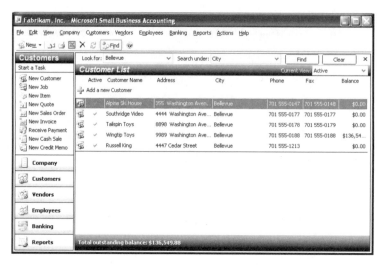

8 To display the complete customer list again, click **Clear**.

9 On the **View** menu, click **Add/Remove Content**.

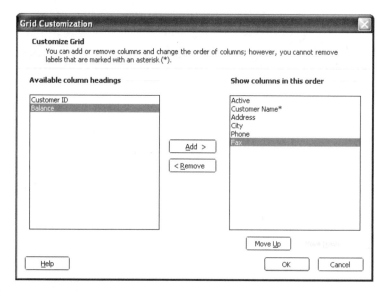

10 In the **Grid Customization** dialog box, in the **Show Columns in This Order** list, click **Fax** and then click **Remove**.

11 To change the order in which the columns appear, in the **Show Columns in this Order** list, click the name of the column you want to move, and then click the **Move Up** or **Move Down** button.

Tip   When you are working with the customer list, you can send an e-mail message to a customer by selecting the customer entry in the list and then clicking the **Email** button on the toolbar.

Creating a Customer Group

Support lists in Small Business Accounting help you organize entities such as customers and vendors and define bookkeeping items such as payment terms and discounts. With customer groups, you might organize customers by city or state or by the volume of business they do. After you have assigned customers to the groups you create, you can view reports based on the groups and examine the similarities and differences in the buying habits of the customers you've grouped together. By analyzing the common details provided by customer groups, you can see trends more quickly and then plan any actions that you need to take.

See Also   You use the **Details** tab on the customer record form to assign a customer to a group. For more information about working with the **Details** tab, see the section "Adding Details to a Customer Record" later in this chapter.

In this exercise, you'll create two customer groups for the Fabrikam sample company. One group is for customers who are individuals, and the second group is for customers that are companies.

OPEN the Fabrikam sample file if you have closed it.

1   On the **Company** menu, point to **Manage Support Lists**, and then click **Customer Group List**.

The **Modify Customer Group** dialog box appears.

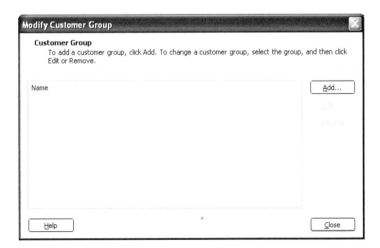

2 Click **Add**.

The **Customer Group** dialog box appears.

3 Type Individual, and click **OK**.

The **Customer Group** dialog box disappears.

4 Click **Add**.

The **Customer Group** dialog box appears.

5 Type Company, and then click **OK**.

6 Click **Close**.

> **Tip** You can change the name of a customer group by selecting the group in the **Modify Customer Group** dialog box and then clicking **Edit**. To delete a customer group, select the group and then click **Remove**. You cannot remove a customer group that you've assigned a customer to.

Creating Price Levels, Credit Ratings, and Payment Terms

In addition to using support lists to group customers, as you learned in the previous exercise, you can use support lists to define pricing, credit, and payment information that you apply to customer accounts.

> **Note** You can edit or remove a price level, credit rating, or payment term to change the definition of the item or to delete it from your company's lists. However, you cannot remove an item if it is assigned to one or more customers.

Defining New Price Levels

A price level is an adjustment to the standard price you charge for the goods and services you sell. For example, for any customer that exceeds a certain volume of sales, you might provide a price level that decreases standard prices by 10 percent. You also might create a list of long-term preferred customers and establish a level that is

15 percent less than standard prices. After you've assigned a price level to a customer, the prices shown when you create a sales order for that customer reflect the adjustment associated with that level.

You define new price levels in the **Add or Edit Price Level** dialog box. By default, the **Decrease Price Level by This Percentage** option is selected. If you want prices to increase by the percentage you've specified, select the **Increase Price Level by This Percentage** option. In most cases, the price levels you create for customers will decrease prices as an incentive to the customer or as a reward for that customer's loyalty. In cases in which a customer orders products infrequently or orders only products that cost you more to manufacture or import, for example, you might apply a price level that increases standard prices.

Defining New Credit Ratings and Payment Terms

Credit ratings are categories that you set up to rank the credit worthiness of customers. You can make up the credit ratings you want to use (something simple like Excellent, Good, Average, and Poor), or you can use or adapt a standard rating scheme. In the Standard & Poor's system, a rating of AAA is given to companies with the highest credit quality. A credit rating of D indicates that a customer has defaulted on a payment.

For a customer that has a specific credit rating or buys a high volume of goods or services, you might provide special payment terms. For example, you might offer a 2 percent reduction if a customer pays within 10 days of receiving a bill. For customers that have fallen behind in their payments, you might insist on payment terms of cash on delivery. Payment terms are assigned to a customer on the **Details** tab of the customer record form. The payment term that you enter in a customer record appears on all sales records for that customer.

Note   In Small Business Accounting you aren't required to assign specific payment terms to a customer. For example, you can select the payment terms you want to use when you create an invoice for each customer. If you do specify payment terms for a customer, those terms will be displayed by default when you create an invoice. You can change the payment terms for a specific invoice before sending it.

Small Business Accounting provides a default set of payment terms, including a 1 percent discount if a payment is made within 10 days, a 2 percent discount with the same terms, Net 15, and Net 30.

Note   The **Payment Terms List** also includes items for taxes that are due monthly, quarterly, and annually.

In this exercise, you'll work again with support lists in Small Business Accounting to create lists of price levels, credit ratings, and payment terms that you can apply to customer accounts.

OPEN the Fabrikam sample file if you have closed it.

1 On the **Company** menu, point to **Manage Support Lists**, and then click **Price Level List**.

The **Modify Price Level** dialog box appears.

2 Click **Add**.

The **Add or Edit Price Level** dialog box appears.

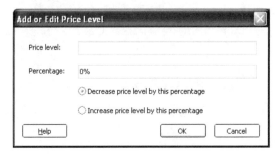

3 In the **Price Level** field, type High-volume customer.

4 In the **Percentage** field, type 10 to adjust these customers' prices by 10 percent.

5 Verify that the **Decrease Price Level by This Percentage** option is selected.

6 Click **OK**, and then click **Close** in the **Modify Price Level** dialog box.

7 On the **Company** menu, point to **Manage Support Lists**, and then click **Credit Rating List**.

The **Modify Credit Rating** dialog box appears.

8 Click **Add**.

The **Credit Rating** dialog box appears.

9 Type Excellent.

10 In the **Credit Rating** dialog box, click **OK**, and then click **Close** in the **Modify Credit Rating** dialog box.

11 On the **Company** menu, point to **Manage Support Lists**, and then click **Payment Terms List**.

The **Modify Payment Term** dialog box appears.

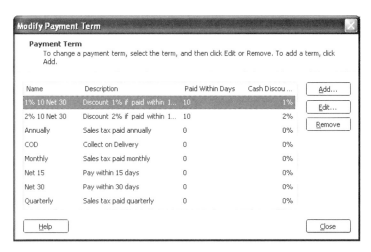

12 In the **Modify Payment Term** dialog box, click **Add**.

The **Payment Term** dialog box appears.

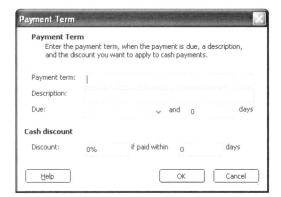

13 In the top portion of the **Payment Term** dialog box, type Net 60, and in the **Description** box, type Pay within 60 days.

14 In the **Due** boxes, type 60 for the number of days.

15 In the **Cash Discount** area of the **Payment Term** dialog box, leave the discount set to **0%** and the days set to **0**.

Note   If you are creating a payment term that provides an incentive for early payment, enter the discount amount and the incentive period in this section of the dialog box.

16 In the **Payment Term** dialog box, click **OK**, and then click **Close** in the **Modify Payment Term** dialog box.

Shipping Terms and Shipping Methods

In addition to payment terms and price levels, many small businesses, especially small manufacturing or retail companies, need to track the shipping method and shipping terms of customer orders. A shipping method might be Via U.S. Post or Via Express. A shipping term describes the agreement you reach with a customer for payment of shipping and handling charges. For example, you might pay for shipping for preferred customers. For first-time customers, you might require shipping charges to be paid cash on delivery.

If you need to define shipping methods and shipping terms for the company you are setting up in Small Business Accounting, point to **Manage Support Lists** on the **Company** menu, and then use the **Shipping Method** or **Shipping Term** command to open the dialog box you need. The steps for creating a shipping method or shipping term are very similar to those described in the previous exercise for creating payment terms.

Setting Up Sales Tax Agencies and Sales Tax Codes

Most of the goods and services that a small business sells are subject to sales tax, and it's likely that most of the customers that a business sells its products and services to are required to pay sales tax. You need to follow several steps to set up Small Business Accounting so that you collect the taxes you need to pay to relevant tax agencies, charge sales tax on the correct items, and charge sales tax to the right customers.

One of the first steps you take is to define the state and local tax agencies you need to remit sales taxes to. For example, if you do business in a state with a sales tax, you need to set up the state tax authority as a tax agency. In addition, if the county and city in which you do business charge sales tax, you need to set up the city and county as tax agencies. You might also need to set up a neighboring county or city as a separate tax agency if your business delivers products to customers in those locations.

You define a new tax agency by opening the **Company** menu, pointing to **Sales Tax**, and then clicking **New Tax Agency** to display the **Tax Agency** dialog box. The fields on the **Tax Agency** dialog box are organized on three tabs. The **General** tab contains defining information about the tax agency. You only need to fill in the **Tax Agency**, **Payment Term**, and **Liability Account** fields to set up a tax agency. You can also enter contact information such as an address, phone numbers, or a Web site for the agency.

The **Financial History** tab displays a list of tax transactions with the agency. On the **Custom Fields** tab, you can define a field you want to use to store additional information about this tax agency.

See Also   For more information about working with custom fields, see the exercise "Creating a Customer Record" earlier in this chapter.

After you define the agencies that you pay sales tax to, you create a *sales tax code* that specifies the name of the sales tax and the amount, which is generally a percentage of the price you charge for the items you sell.

Tip   Tax rates change from time to time as states and cities adjust them. If you know the tax rate will increase or decrease on a given date in the future, update the rate for the tax code ahead of time and enter the effective date of the rate change. That way, when you generate invoices and sales orders later, the correct tax rate will be applied to those transactions.

In this exercise, you'll enter information for a tax agency and then create a sales tax code associated with the agency. The form you use to create a tax agency is similar to the customer record form. You enter the agency's name, address, and other contact information and details about the tax account.

OPEN the Fabrikam sample file if you have closed it.

1   On the **Company** menu, point to **Sales Tax**, and then click **New Tax Agency**.

The **Tax Agency** dialog box appears.

2   In the **Tax Agency** box, type Washington State.

3   Under **Account Information**, in the **Payment Term** list, click **Quarterly**.

4   In the **Liability Account** list, click **Sales Tax Payable**.

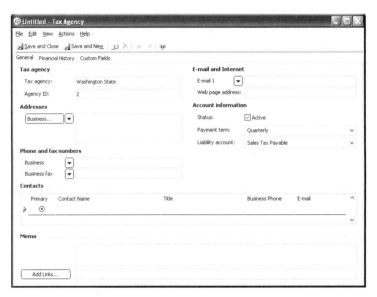

5 Complete the contact information you want to enter for the tax agency, and then click **Save and Close**.

The **Tax Agency** dialog box disappears.

6 On the **Company** menu, point to **Sales Tax**, and then click **Manage Sales Tax Codes**.

The **Manage Tax Code Name** dialog box appears.

7 Click **Add**.

8 In the **Add or Edit Tax Code** dialog box, in the **Tax Code** box, type King County.

9 In the **Tax Agency** list, click **Washington State**.

10 In the **Tax Settings: Rate** area, type 3.2. Then, in the **As of** field, type 7/1/2005.

11   In the **Add or Edit Tax Code** dialog box, click **OK**, and then click **Close** in the **Modify Tax Code Name** dialog box.

Creating Sales Tax Groups

As part of creating a customer record, you assign a sales tax group to a customer. A sales tax group is made up of one or more sales tax codes. For example, a sales tax group might include the sales tax codes for a state taxing agency, the county tax assessor, and a city tax agency.

You need to set up a sales tax group to account for the tax status of different types of customers. For example, some customers might be exempt from paying taxes because the customer is a not-for-profit organization. Determining the tax group that you assign to a customer is based on factors such as the customer's location and whether the customer purchases items on-site at your store or warehouse or whether you deliver purchased goods to the customer.

In this exercise, you'll learn how to create a sales tax group. Each sales tax group is named and then defined by adding the sales tax codes that apply.

OPEN the Fabrikam sample file if you have closed it.

1   On the **Company** menu, point to **Sales Tax**, and then click **Manage Sales Tax Groups**.

The **Modify Sales Tax Group** dialog box appears.

2   Click **Add**.

The **Tax Group** dialog box appears.

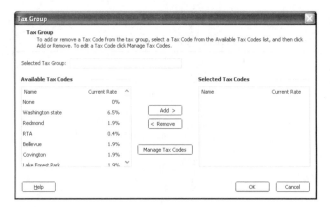

3 In the **Selected Tax Group** box, type King County Businesses.

4 In the **Available Tax Codes** list, click King County, and then click **Add**. If more than one new tax applies to the group, you can repeat this step to add any other applicable tax codes.

Your changes appear in the **Tax Group** dialog box.

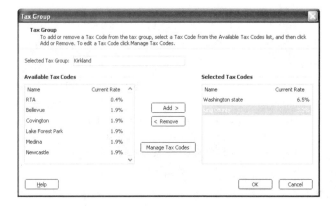

Tip If you need to edit a tax code—for example, update the tax percentage—while you are working in the **Tax Group** dialog box, click **Manage Tax Codes**.

5 Click **OK**, and then click **Close** in the **Modify Sales Tax Group** dialog box.

Adding Details to a Customer Record

In the first exercise in this chapter, when you created a customer record, you learned how to add contact information for a customer and how to create a field in which you can store customer information of your choice. In addition to storing contact information and viewing financial summaries in a customer record, you can use a customer record in Small Business Accounting to specify customer account details such as the credit rating, pricing level, and payment terms that apply to a customer's account. You specify these settings on the **Details** tab.

One of the details you can add to your customer is their preferred shipping method. Some customers are willing to pay for expedited delivery, but most customers are content to use a lower-priced alternative. Companies that manufacture or sell finished goods should define a set of shipping methods, but small service companies might not require this information.

See Also   For more information about shipping methods and shipping terms, see the sidebar "Shipping Terms and Shipping Methods" earlier in this chapter.

Another detail you can add to a customer's record is their credit limit. The amount of the credit limit should correspond to the credit rating.

Important   You should periodically review the credit limits for your list of customers to see whether any should be revised.

In this exercise, you will add account details to a customer record. The settings you specify on the **Details** tab for an item such as a customer's payment terms or price level are reflected in forms such as invoices, quotes, and purchase orders. You can, however, override these settings for individual orders or transactions when you need to.

OPEN the Fabrikam sample file if you have closed it.

1   On the **Customers** menu, point to **Customer Lists**, and then click **Customers**.

The **Customer List** appears.

2   Double-click **City Power & Light**, and then click the **Details** tab.

The **Details** tab of the customer record form appears.

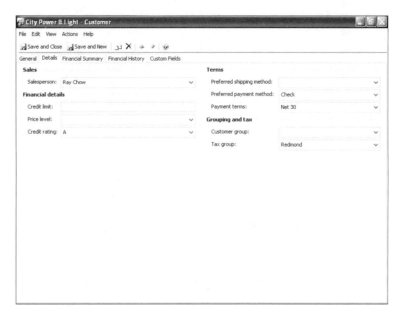

3 Click the **Salesperson** down arrow, and then click **Karen Archer**.

Note The salesperson list is created when you enter employees into Small Business Accounting. For more information about working with employee records in Small Business Accounting, see Chapter 12, "Managing Employee Time and Payroll."

4 In the **Credit Limit** box, type 10000.

5 Click the **Credit Rating** down arrow and then click **A+**.

6 Click the **Preferred Shipping Method** down arrow, and then click **Add a New Shipping Method**.

The **Shipping Method** dialog box appears.

7 Click the **Shipping Method** down arrow and then click **Mail**.

8 Click the **Preferred Payment Method,** and then click **Credit Card**. You can leave the **Payment Terms** value at the default value of **Net 30**.

Tip   If you want to create a payment term when you are filling in a customer record, click **Add a New Payment Term** at the top of the list and then enter the details in the **Payment Terms** dialog box. You can create a credit rating, price level, or similar item in the same manner.

9   In the **Tax Group** list, click **None**.

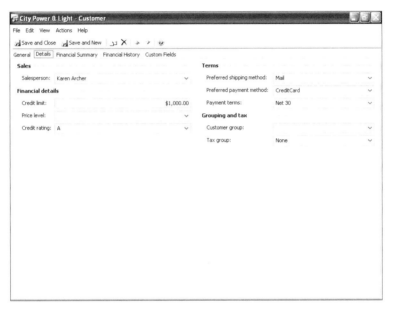

10   Click **Save and Close**. If you want to save this customer record and start working with a blank record, click **Save and New**.

Tip   You can advance from customer record to customer record by clicking the **Previous** or **Next** button on the toolbar.

Creating a Record for a Tax-exempt Customer

Some of the customers that you work with will be exempt from paying sales tax, for example, a nonprofit organization or a customer located out of state. When creating a customer record in Small Business Accounting, you can indicate whether a customer is exempt from taxes and also specify the reason for the tax exemption for your official financial records. When you create a quote or process another transaction with the customer, no taxes are charged. You should create a sales tax group and a sales tax code for each type of tax exemption. You can then apply this tax group to the customer's record when you are working on the **Details** tab.

Creating a Customer Statement Template

Small Business Accounting includes templates that you can use for invoices, sales orders, purchase orders, customer statements, and other business documents. The templates are designed in Microsoft Office Word. Like other templates, these forms help keep the information you present to customers and vendors consistent and professional in appearance. Using the templates enables you to avoid the need to create and format every document you send individually.

A customer statement template should include fields that display your company name and address, the customer's contact information, and the data from the financial transactions that the statement summarizes. When you create a template in Word, or if you want to modify one of the templates that come with Small Business Accounting, you can add or remove fields, design the layout of the template, and apply formatting in Word to specify fonts and other elements you want to use on the template.

The accounting templates you design in Word are created using the *XML (Extensible Markup Language)*, which is a data transfer and document markup technology that is used in a variety of ways in Microsoft Office applications. The XML tags you add to the Word template correspond to the customer, company, and financial fields in Small Business Accounting. When you create statements, Small Business Accounting and Word communicate through the use of XML. You can display the XML tags in Word, but clearing the check box can make it easier to lay out the template in Word.

The Microsoft Word **Document Actions** pane lists the fields that can be used in the template. You add fields to the template in a manner similar to setting up fields for a form letter or mailing labels when working with the mail merge feature in Word. The fields are organized into groups related to customer information, company information, and header fields. There is also a field named **Line**, which inserts financial information about a customer transaction into documents created from the template.

In this exercise, you will set up a customer statement template that you can use to summarize account activity.

OPEN the Fabrikam sample file if you have closed it.

1 On the **Company** menu, click **Manage Word Templates**.

The **Manage Microsoft Word Templates** dialog box appears.

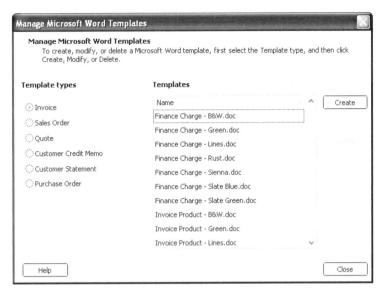

2 In the **Template Types** list, click **Customer Statement**, and then click **Create**.

The **Create New Microsoft Word Template** dialog box appears.

Tip To base your customer statement on one of the templates that come with Small Business Accounting, select the statement template in the **Templates** list, and then click **Modify**.

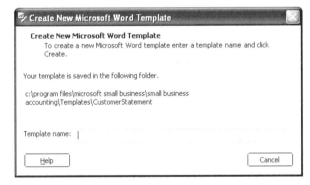

3 In the **Create New Microsoft Word Template** dialog box, type Fabrikam_Customer_Statement.

4 Click **Create**.

The new **Fabrikam_Customer_Statement** template appears in a Word window.

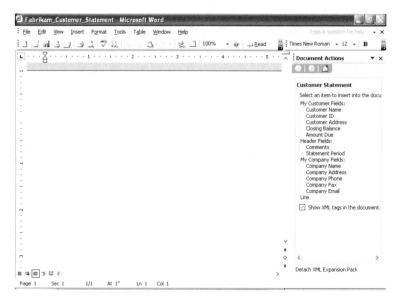

5 In the **Document Actions** task pane, ensure that the **Show XML Tags in the Document** check box is selected.

6 Click **Statement Period** to add that information to the top of the document.

Tip The customer statement templates that come with Small Business Accounting are set up as tables in Word. A table helps keep the fields you add aligned and positioned in the document. You can adjust the width of the columns and rows in the table to match the amount of text a particular table cell needs to contain.

7 Click to the right of the closing **StatementPeriod** XML tag.

8 In the **Document Actions** task pane, click the other customer contact fields (**Customer ID**, **Customer Name**, and **Customer Address**) to add this information to the top of the document.

9 Use the [Enter] key to add three blank lines to the document.

10 In the **Document Actions** pane, click **Line**.

The **Line** field adds several detailed transaction fields to the statement. The fields include the data of each transaction, the type of transaction, the transaction number, the due date, the payment status, the amount, and the balance.

11 After the **Line** field, use the **Document Actions** pane to add the **Closing Balance** field and the **Amount Due** field to the customer statement.

12 At the bottom of the document, type the text Thank you for your business or some similar message to your customers.

13 In the **Document Actions** pane, in the **My Company Fields** area, add the fields for your company contact information to the statement.

14 In Word, on the **File** menu, click **Save**.

Word saves your template.

15 In Word, on the **File** menu, click **Exit**.

The Word template disappears.

CLOSE the Fabrikam sample file.

Key Points

- The **Customers** home page is a centralized location from which you can work with customer records and customer transactions.

- Customer records store contact information in addition to account details. Customer records also provide a view of a customer's financial history.

- You can sort the customer list by fields such as **City** and **Balance**.

- Support lists let you create and define administrative tools such as company groups, credit ratings, payment terms, pricing levels, and tax groups.

- The accounting templates that come with Small Business Accounting help organize and present the information you provide to customers and review yourself.

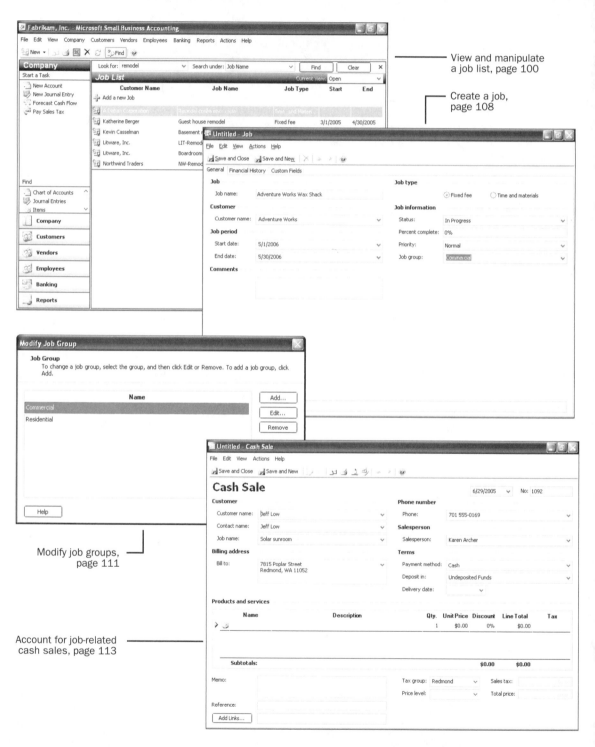

View and manipulate
a job list, page 100

Create a job,
page 108

Modify job groups,
page 111

Account for job-related
cash sales, page 113

Chapter 6 at a Glance

6 Managing Jobs

In this chapter you will learn to:

✔ Define a job.

✔ View and manipulate the job list.

✔ Create a job.

✔ Edit jobs.

✔ Create job groups.

✔ Account for job-related cash sales.

Retail stores sell items, but when your company builds houses, repairs cars, or builds information systems, you need a way to track every payment and expenditure related to the project. In Microsoft Office Small Business Accounting 2006, you can create a single entity allowing you to record everything related to your project. That entity, called a *job*, gives you places to enter information about the customer, the job's start and end dates, and the transactions related to the job.

In this chapter, you will learn how to define a job, view and manipulate the job list, create a new job, edit information about existing jobs, and assign cash transactions to existing jobs.

See Also   Do you need only a quick refresher on the topics in this chapter? See the Quick Reference entries on pages xxvi–xxvii.

What Is a Job?

In Small Business Accounting, a *job* represents a multi-part project made up of products and services you deliver over time. For example, if a ski resort's general manager asked Fabrikam to build a ski waxing and maintenance facility at their trail base, Fabrikam would create a job for the ski resort in its Small Business Accounting file and then respond with a quote that would be linked to that job.

See Also For more information on creating a job based on an existing quote, see Chapter 7, "Generating and Managing Quotes."

Enabling Jobs in Small Business Accounting

To use jobs in Small Business Accounting, you must have the **Use Job** check box selected in your company preferences. If you aren't sure whether you enabled jobs in your company's file, click **Preferences** on the **Company** menu, and on the **Company** tab of the **Company Preferences** dialog box, make sure the **Use Job** check box is selected.

Types of Jobs

There are two basic job types in Small Business Accounting: a *fixed fee job* and a *time and materials job*. A fixed fee job is just what the name implies: a job your company agrees to complete for a set price. The other job type, the time and materials job, charges the customer for the labor and supplies used to complete the project, plus a markup for your profit. You will usually prepare a quote for the customer; if the customer accepts your quote and you sign a contract, you may then start work. Once you begin work on a job, you can track the time it takes and expenditures you make to complete the job. For example, if Fabrikam purchases lumber with which to build a shed, the company can link those purchases to the job. Whenever you create a purchase order; buy an item by using cash, check, or charge; or subcontract service items to another provider, you can assign the cost to the job for which you're making the purchase. You can assign service items, including time spent by your employees working on the job, by clicking the **Job Name** down arrow in the appropriate window and selecting the job to which you want to assign the costs.

Viewing the Job List

Small Business Accounting stores all of your jobs in a single list, the job list. To display the job list, open the **Company** menu in the Fabrikam sample file, point to **Company Lists**, and then click **Jobs**.

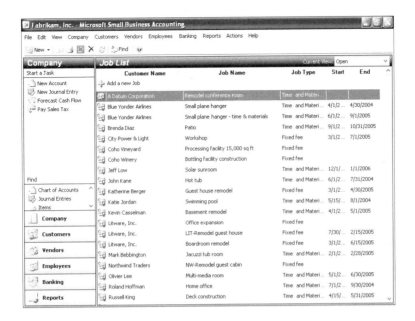

Manipulating the Job List

If you've been in business for a while, it's very likely that your **Job List** contains a lot of entries. Small Business Accounting enables you to rearrange and limit the data that appears in the **Job List**, making it easier for you to find the job entry you're looking for.

Each **Job List** column header has three sorting options:

■ Unsorted displays the jobs in the order in which they were entered into the program.

■ Sorted in ascending order sorts the list by placing the jobs with the lowest values in the selected field at the top of the list. For example, sorting the **Start** field in ascending order would put a job with a start date of 2/9/2006 above a job with a start date of 8/2/2006.

■ Sorted in descending order sorts the list by placing the jobs with the highest values in the clicked field at the top of the list. For example, sorting the **Start** field in descending order would put a job with a start date of 8/2/2006 above a job with a start date of 2/9/2006.

Clicking the header of an unsorted column sorts the **Job List** in ascending order based on the contents of that column; clicking the header again sorts the **Job List** in descending order based on the contents of that column; and clicking the header a third time restores the column and the **Job List** to their original order. If you'd like to sort the list based on the values in more than one column, such as by **Customer Name** first and then by **Job Name**, hold down the [Ctrl] key and then click the column headers in the order by which you would like the list to be sorted.

If you're having trouble finding a job you want to view, you can locate just those jobs that contain a specific value in either the **Customer Name**, **Job Name**, or **Job Type** column. For example, if you want to filter the **Job List** so that it contains only those jobs that have the word *remodel* in the **Job Name** field, click the **Find** button on the toolbar. Clicking the **Find** button displays the **Find** toolbar.

In the **Look for** field, type the value you want to look up. Then, click the **Search under** down arrow and click the field in which you want to search. When you've set your criteria, click the **Find** button on the **Find** toolbar to display just those records where your search term occurs in the field you designated.

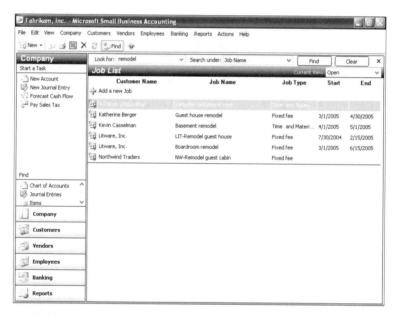

Clicking the **Find** button on the Small Business Accounting program's main toolbar removes an active filter and hides the **Find** toolbar. If you'd rather remove the current filter but keep the **Find** toolbar open, click the **Clear** button.

In this exercise you will manipulate the **Job List** to display just the jobs you want to view.

BE SURE TO start Small Business Accounting if it is not already running.

OPEN the Fabrikam sample file.

1 On the **Company** menu, point to **Company Lists** and then click **Jobs**.

The **Job List** appears.

2 Click the **Customer Name** column header.

Small Business Accounting sorts Fabrikam's **Job List** in descending order by using the values in the **Customer Name** column.

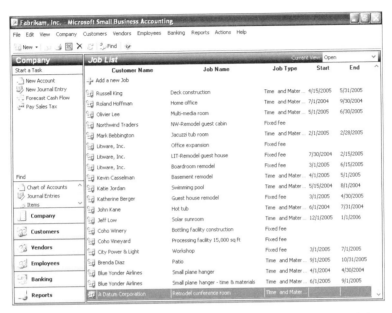

3 Hold down [Ctrl] and click the **Customer Name** column header and then the **Job Name** column header to select both columns, in that order.

Small Business Accounting sorts the **Job List** using the values in the **Customer Name** column as its primary sorting criteria, using the values in the **Job Name** column to determine a sort order for jobs that have the same value in the **Customer Name** column.

4 On the toolbar, click the **Find** button.

The **Find** toolbar appears above the **Job List**.

5 In the **Look for** field, type office.

6 Click the **Search Under** down arrow and then click **Job Name**.

7 Click the **Find** button.

Small Business Accounting displays the two jobs that contain the term *office* in the **Job Name** field.

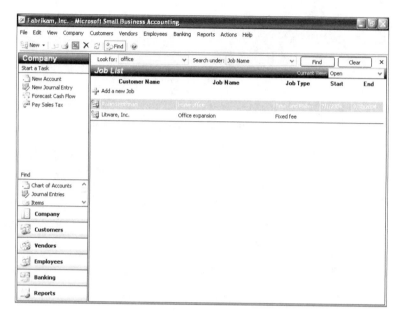

8 Click the **Clear** button on the **Find** toolbar.

Small Business Accounting removes the filter from the **Job List**.

9 On the main toolbar, click the **Find** button.

The **Find** toolbar disappears.

Viewing the Job List by Job Status

Managing a company requires that you know how your projects are progressing. It's important to know which of your job offers were not accepted, how many projects you have going for a given client at any one time, and whether you have a lot of projects that are due to start in the near future.

To help you capture that information, Small Business Accounting lets you assign jobs to five status categories:

- **Open** indicates that a job listing has been created for the project but that the job has not yet been completed or canceled.

- **In Progress** indicates that a job has been started but has not been completed.

- **Completed** indicates that a job has been started and finished.

- **Not Started** indicates that a job has been created but that work has not begun.

- **All** lists every job regardless of its status.

In this exercise you will filter the **Job List** by job status.

OPEN the Fabrikam sample file if you have closed it.

1   On the **Company** menu, point to **Company Lists,** and then click **Jobs**.

The **Job List** appears.

2   Click the **Current View** down arrow and then click **In Progress**.

Small Business Accounting filters the **Job List** so it shows just those projects that are in progress.

3   On the main program toolbar, click the **Find** button.

The **Find** toolbar appears above the **Job List**.

4   In the **Look For** field, type remodel.

5   Click the **Search Under** down arrow and then click **Job Name**.

6   Click **Find**.

The **Job List** displays only those remodeling efforts that are in progress.

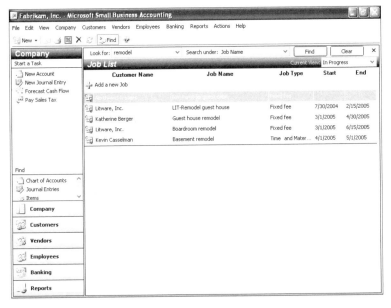

7   On the main program toolbar, click **Find**.

The **Find** toolbar disappears and the program removes the filter from the **Job List**.

8   Click the **Current View** down arrow and then click **Open**.

Small Business Accounting displays jobs for which a quote has been generated and that have not been completed or canceled.

Viewing Job Details

If you want to view a job's details, double-click anywhere on the job's row. When you do, a job form appears.

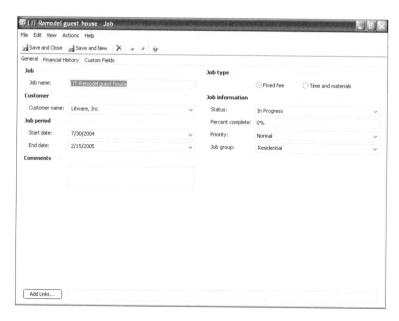

Tip   While you are viewing a job's details, you can display the next job in the **Job List** by clicking the **Next Item** button on the toolbar. To display the previous job in the list, click the **Previous Item** button.

Each job form has three tabs: **General**, **Financial History**, and **Custom Fields**. The **General** tab contains fields such as the job name, customer for whom the job will be performed, whether the job is a fixed fee or time and materials job, and the job's status.

Clicking the **Financial History** tab displays every transaction related to a job, including the original quote (if any), all purchases made in relation to the project, and all invoices sent to the customer.

See Also   For information on creating progress invoices, which are requests for partial payment as a job progresses, see Chapter 9, "Preparing and Managing Invoices."

The **Custom Fields** tab contains the **Customize** button, which you can click to display the **Customize Form** dialog box. The **Custom Fields** tab also lists any custom fields you've created to help you track your jobs.

See Also   For more information on custom fields, and to work through an exercise that shows you how to create custom fields, see Chapter 4, "Managing Products and Services." The procedure for creating custom fields for jobs is the same for jobs as it is for products and services.

In this exercise you will view a job's details, including its financial history.

OPEN the Fabrikam sample file if you have closed it.

1   On the **Customers** menu, click **Customers Home**.

The **Customers** home page appears.

2   In the **Find** section at the bottom of the **Customers** page, click **Jobs**.

The **Job List** appears.

3   Scroll through the **Job List** and double-click the job for customer **Wilson Pais**.

The **Steam Bath** job form appears.

4   Click the **Financial History** tab.

The **Financial History** tab appears.

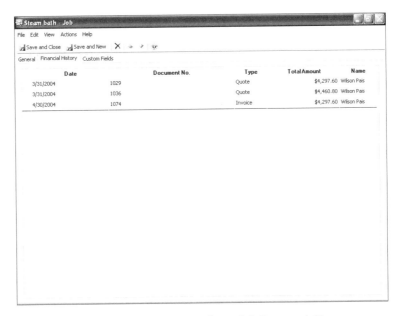

5   On the **Steam Bath - Job** form's toolbar, click **Save and Close**.

The **Steam Bath** job form disappears.

6   On the **Company** menu, click **Company Home**.

The Fabrikam home page appears.

Creating Jobs

When you're ready to create a job, you can do so by opening the **Customers** menu and then clicking **Customers Home** to display the **Customers** home page. Once you are on the **Customers** home page, you can click the **New Job** item to open up a job form and enter the details of your new job.

In this exercise you will create a job.

OPEN the Fabrikam sample file if you have closed it.

1   On the **Customers** menu, click **Customers Home**.

The **Customers** home page appears.

2   In the **More Tasks** section of the **Customers** page, click **New Job**.

An untitled job form appears.

3   In the **Job Name** field, type Adventure Works Wax Shack.

4   Click the **Customer Name** down arrow and then click **Adventure Works**.

5   In the **Start Date** field, type 5/1/2006.

6   In the **End Date** field, type 5/30/2006.

7   In the **Job Type** area of the form, select the **Fixed Fee** option.

8   Leave the **Percent Complete**, **Status**, and **Priority** field values at the default (**Normal** priority, **In Progress** status, and **0%** complete).

9 Click the **Job Group** down arrow and then click **Commercial**.

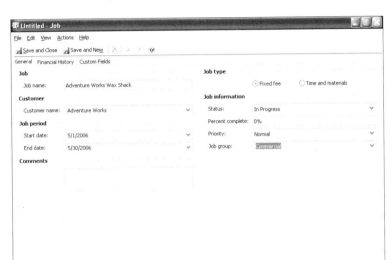

10 On the toolbar, click the **Save and Close** button.

The job form disappears.

Editing and Deleting Jobs

Circumstances change in every industry, regardless of whether it's the construction industry (the home industry of our fictitious Fabrikam), automobile sales, or software programming. The bid you submit for a job may or may not be successful. You could enter incorrect information about a job, perhaps assigning it to the wrong customer, and need to fix your listing. Finally, you might hear back from a potential client that they're not going forward with a project, which means that you can safely delete the job you added to your company file.

To change a job's information, just display the job's information on screen and edit the values that need editing. For example, you might change a job's status from **Open** to **In Progress**. You could also change the project's start or end date if the client needs you to start or finish the project at a time other than the one you first entered into the job.

Deleting a job is a straightforward but final operation that you should only undertake if there are no other documents related to the job in your company file. You should also consider keeping all of your jobs around. For example, if you maintain a record of unconsummated deals, when a potential client contacts you about possible projects but never follows through with an offer of work, you might consider changing how you handle requests for proposals from that client in the future.

In this exercise you will modify and then delete a job.

OPEN the Fabrikam sample file if you have closed it.

1 On the **Customers** menu, point to **Customers Lists** and then click **Jobs**.

The **Job List** appears.

2 Double-click the job named **Adventure Works Wax Shack**.

The **Adventure Works Wax Shack** job appears.

Note You created the Adventure Works Wax Shack job in an exercise earlier in this chapter. If you didn't create that job, or if you don't want to edit or delete it, move through this exercise but don't save your changes or delete the job you use.

3 In the **Start Date** field, change the date to 6/1/2006.

4 In the **End Date** field, change the date to 6/30/2006.

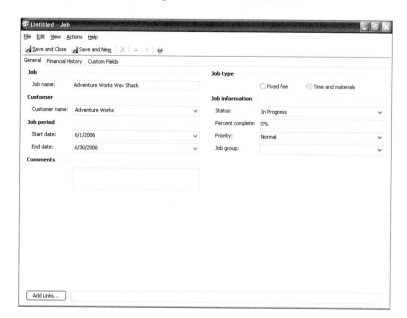

5   In the **Job Type** area of the form, select the **Time and Materials** option.

6   On the **File** menu, click **Close** and click **No** when you're asked if you want to save your changes.

The job form disappears.

7   On the main toolbar, click the **Delete** button.

A confirmation dialog box appears.

8   Click **Yes** to confirm that you want to delete the selected job.

Modifying Job Groups

When you create a company file, Small Business Accounting assumes all of your projects should be considered together when you generate reports to analyze your business performance. If you would like to distinguish one set of jobs from the other jobs undertaken by your company, you can do so by creating a new job group. The Fabrikam sample company file, for example, contains two job groups: commercial and residential. By setting up separate groups, you can use the **Profitability by Job Summary** report to compare Fabrikam's commercial and residential projects.

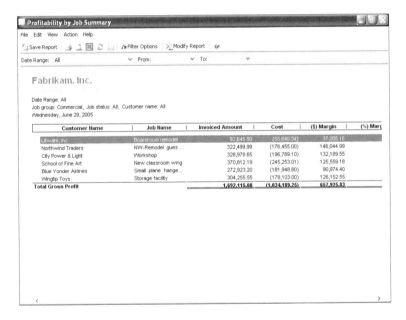

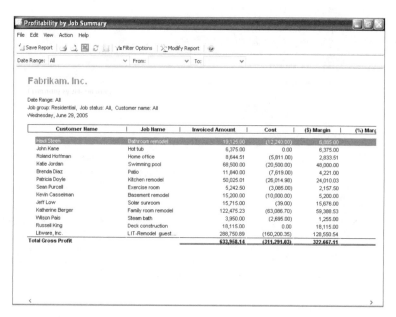

You can create a new job group by opening the **Company** menu, pointing to **Manage Support Lists**, and then clicking **Job Group List**. When you do, the **Modify Job Group** dialog box appears.

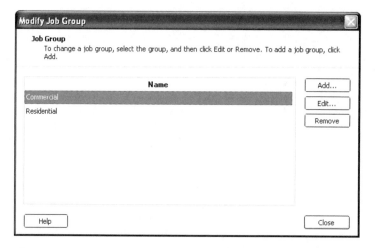

The **Name** list displays all of the available job group names. You can then click the **Add** button to create a new group, click the **Edit** button to change information about an existing group, or click the **Remove** button to delete a group entirely.

In this exercise you will create a new group for Fabrikam jobs.

OPEN the Fabrikam sample file if you have closed it.

1 On the **Company** menu, point to **Manage Support Lists**, and then click **Job Group List**.

The **Modify Job Group** dialog box appears.

2 Click **Add**.

The **Job Group** dialog box appears.

3 In the **Job Group Name** field, type Aviation.

4 Click **OK**.

The **Job Group** dialog box disappears, and the **Aviation** job group appears in the **Modify Job Group** dialog box.

5 Click **Close**.

The **Modify Job Group** dialog box disappears.

Accounting for Cash Sales Related to a Job

Handling cash purchases is difficult for any company. Cash is messy, cash is hard to keep track of, and employees always seem to lose the receipt they need to submit to deduct an expense on your corporate taxes. Those considerations aside, Small Business Accounting attempts to make assigning cash transactions to a particular job as straightforward as possible.

In this exercise you will assign a cash sale to a job.

OPEN the Fabrikam sample file if you have closed it.

1 In the **Navigation Pane**, click **Customers**.

The **Customers** home page appears.

2 Under **Find**, click **Jobs**.

The **Jobs List** appears.

3 Click the **Solar sunroom** project for **Jeff Low**.

4 On the **Actions** menu, click **Create Cash Sales**.

A **Cash Sale** form appears.

5 In the **Products and Services** pane, click the **Name** field on the active row.

6 Click the down arrow that appears in the **Name** field and then click **Carpentry (TM)**.

7 Click the **Save and Close** button on the toolbar.

See Also For information on assigning a purchase order to a job, see Chapter 11, "Purchasing from and Paying Vendors."

Key Points

- Creating jobs enables you to store all products and services related to a project in a single entity.

- You can sort and filter the job list to make it easier to find the jobs you are looking for.

- The job form has a **Financial History** tab, on which you can find every transaction related to the job.

- You can assign your jobs to a job group, which enables you to create reports for each job group (e.g., all commercial construction jobs as compared to all residential construction jobs).

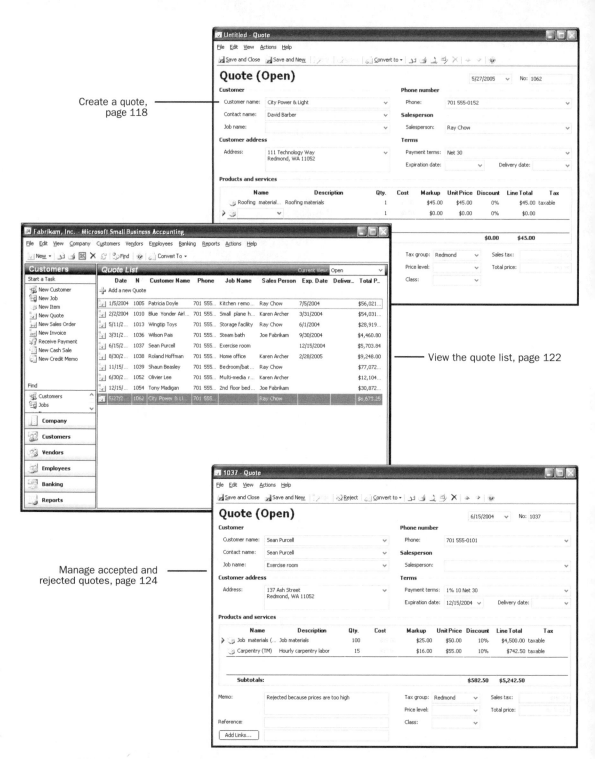

Create a quote, page 118

View the quote list, page 122

Manage accepted and rejected quotes, page 124

Chapter 7 at a Glance

7 Generating and Managing Quotes

In this chapter you will learn to:

✔ Create a quote.

✔ View the list of quotes.

✔ Manage accepted and rejected quotes.

✔ Create quote templates.

In a small business such as an engineering or architectural firm, a general contractor, or a small manufacturer, customers often require that the company provide an estimate of the costs of products and services before the customer commits to a purchase. Likewise, a small business needs to be clear about the products and services it agrees to provide, what it will charge for those items, and when the work is due.

In Microsoft Office Small Business Accounting 2006, a *quote* specifies the products and services you agree to sell or provide to a customer, what those items will cost, and the delivery date of a proposed transaction. In addition to price information, a quote specifies discounts, shipping information, and *payment terms*. A quote also specifies its expiration date to define the time period for which the terms of the quote are valid.

You build a quote in Small Business Accounting from the list of products and services set up for your company as *items*. For example, a quote might list all the plumbing parts you need for a job plus the labor required to complete the work. Or a quote might list a series of tasks for a landscaping job with the hourly rates and time required to complete each task. A quote can also be associated with a job that you define in Small Business Accounting. For complex jobs, you might provide a quote for different phases of the job.

When you create a quote, the status of the quote is open. The customer that receives the quote can then notify you whether it is accepted or rejected, or the quote can simply expire if the expiration date passes without the customer taking action. A quote that a customer accepts serves as the basis for an invoice or a sales order for the goods and services described in the quote. A quote that a customer rejects might represent only a lost business opportunity, but you can also revise a rejected quote based on feedback you solicit from the customer and submit the quote again.

In this chapter, you will learn how to create a quote and how to manage a quote once a customer has accepted or rejected it. You will also learn how to view the list of quotes and how to gain some helpful insights about your business by sorting and filtering the quote list.

See Also Do you need only a quick refresher on the topics in this chapter? See the Quick Reference entries on pages xxvii–xxviii.

Creating a Quote

Preparing a quote is part business operation and part customer relationship. For example, quotes have expiration dates. In setting the expiration date for a quote, you might need to take several factors into account, such as cost of goods you are reselling or using for manufacturing for a customer. If your supplier can guarantee a price for 30 days, a quote based on this price should expire in an equivalent period of time; otherwise you risk losing part of your profit.

In addition, although not all prospective business transactions require that you provide a quote, many small businesses operate in competitive environments, and their customers request proposals from more than one company before deciding which company to use. A quote that details the financial terms of a business transaction might be part of a larger presentation prepared in response to a formal request for a proposal, or RFP. At other times, a quote is simply good practice so that you as the seller and the customer as the buyer agree to the terms of a sale before the deal is closed.

Initiating a Quote

When you initiate a quote by filling out a quote form, the quote's status is **Open**. The status is displayed beside the main label at the top of the form. Small Business Accounting fills in the current date and assigns a number to the quote, but both can be modified. For example, you can change the date to reflect the date on which you submit the quote (assuming you work on the quote for more than one day) or to reflect the date of a meeting you have with the customer. You can change the quote number to conform to a numbering system you've set up for your company.

The upper half of the quote form displays contact information for the customer and the payment terms, expiration date, and delivery date. You use the **Products and Services** area of the form to specify each line item included in the quote. Each line item includes the name and a description of the item, the quantity, price, and other details.

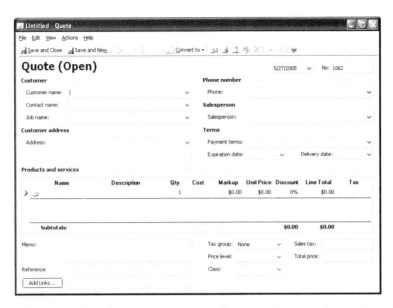

When you select the customer's name from the **Customer Name** list, other contact fields are filled in based on the customer's record. These fields include the principal contact person for this customer, the business address and phone number, and the salesperson assigned to the customer's account. If the customer's record specifies default payment terms, the **Payment Terms** field is filled in. You can change the payment terms for this particular quote if you need to.

At the bottom of the quote form, the **Tax Group** that this customer belongs to is displayed. (If a customer has not been assigned to a tax group, the field is blank.) As the quote is built, the sales tax rates are applied to the price of line items. These rates are defined in the tax codes that are included in the tax group.

Adding Line Items to a Quote

The products and services listed are mostly those you have set up as *items*. The description of the item comes from the item's record. If you type a name of an item that is not included in the list of products and services, Small Business Accounting prompts you to add it to the list before you continue creating the quote.

Most of the line items in a quote are products and services defined in a company's item list. A line item can also refer to an account in a company's chart of accounts, indicate a sales tax that applies to the quote, or provide a comment on a line item or another aspect of the quote. To change the type of a line item, click the icon in the first cell of the line item row, and then select the type of line item you want to use: **Item**, **Comment**, **Sales Tax**, or **Account**.

When you add a line item to a quote, the **Cost** and **Unit Price** fields are filled in using the details in the item record. The **Cost** field in the quote is the standard cost defined in the item's record. The **Unit Price** field is the sales price defined in the item's record. Small Business Accounting calculates the dollar value of the **Markup** field by subtracting the cost from the unit price. **Line Total** is calculated as a product of **Quantity** and **Unit Price**.

You can change the markup and unit price in the quote to balance your company's profit with the overall cost of the quote to the customer. When you change one of these fields, Small Business Accounting recalculates the values in the others and adjusts the line total, sales tax, and overall total for the quote.

In this exercise, you will create a quote in Small Business Accounting using one of the customers in the Fabrikam sample company. You will specify line items in the quote using the list of products and services, and learn how you can adjust prices and discounts while creating a quote. You'll also add a comment to a line item in a quote, and you'll see the steps and calculations that Small Business Accounting performs for you when you prepare a quote.

OPEN the Fabrikam sample file.

1 On the **Navigation** pane, click **Customers**.

The **Customers** home page appears.

2 Under **Start a Task**, click **New Quote**.

3 Click the **Customer Name** down arrow, and then click **City Power and Light**.

Small Business Accounting populates the customer's information into the quote form.

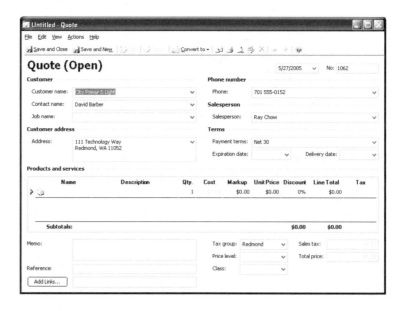

See Also For information about creating customer records and about defining tax groups and tax codes, see Chapter 5, "Setting Up Customer Information."

> **Note** If you select the **Use Jobs** option in the **Company Preferences** dialog box, the quote form includes the **Job Name** field. You can create a quote for a fixed fee or a time and materials job. If you select the **Use Class** option as a company preference, the quote form includes the **Class** field. You can use this field to include which class a quote belongs to. For example, if you have set up sales regions as classes, you can designate the region in the quote.

4 In the **Expiration Date** field, type 3/25/2006.

5 In the **Delivery Date** field, type 4/1/2006.

6 Under **Products and Services**, click in the **Name** column, click the down arrow that appears, and then click **Roofing Materials (FF)**.

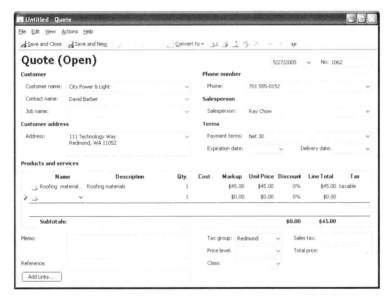

7 In the **Description** field, modify the default description or enter a new one.

8 Click the **Item** icon at the far left of the second row, and then click **Comment**.

9 In the **Description** field, type Grade A materials; Color: Sage.

10 In the **Qty.** (quantity) field, type 124.

11 In the **Discount** field, type 2.5.

Tip To apply a discount to the total amount of the quote rather than to a single line item, add an **Account** line item to the quote, specify the **Discount** expense account, and then enter the amount of the discount in the **Unit Price** field.

12 In the row below the comment you entered, click in the **Name** column and then click **Roofing Labor**.

13 In the **Qty.** field, type 40.

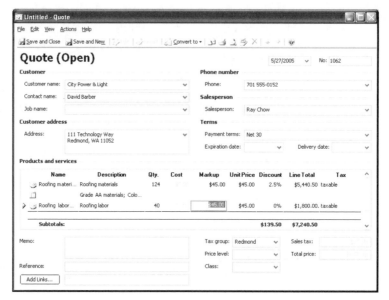

14 In the **Price level** list, click **Preferred Customer**.

Small Business Accounting applies the Preferred Customer discount to the quoted prices.

15 Click **Save and Close**.

Viewing the Quote List

If you use Small Business Accounting to manage a company that provides quotes to customers, you should regularly review the list of quotes. You use the list of quotes to manage the status of the quotes you have provided to customers and to gain information about the quotes the company provides. For example, you can sort the list of quotes by expiration date to see which quotes are due to expire soon. You can then follow up with each customer or with the salesperson assigned to the customer's account to determine whether the customer has made a decision about the quote.

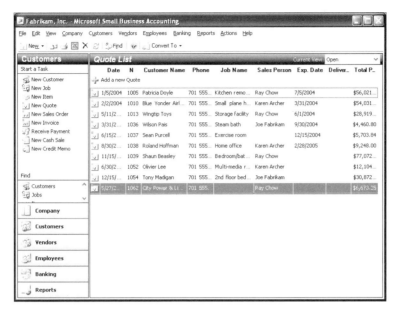

Also, by reviewing the quote list you gain information that can provide insights into your business. Viewing the list of quotes that have been rejected, for example, might reveal patterns about why your company wasn't awarded a job or a sale. Does a particular item you sell or service you provide appear frequently on rejected quotes? Does that mean that the price you charge for this item or service is not in line with your competitors' prices? Which of your goods and services are more often included on successful quotes? By sorting the quote list by salesperson, you can see which of the sales staff have generated more quotes and which of the salespeople have their quotes accepted the majority of the time.

By default, the quote list displays **Open** quotes—those quotes that a customer has not yet accepted or rejected. The quote list displays a summary of information about each quote, including the customer's name and phone number, the related job name, the sales person, the expiration and delivery dates, and the amount of the quote.

In addition to viewing all quotes, you can use the **Current View** list to filter the list to show quotes that have a particular status—**Open**, **Accepted**, **Rejected**, or **Expired**. Switching the view of the quote list is a simple way to gather information about possible trends in your business. For example, click **Expired** in the **Current View** list, and you can see how many quotes have expired in the past 2 weeks, 30 days, or 6 months. Did the quotes that you provided for a particular customer always expire? If so, should you continue providing quotes to this customer or does this customer need some additional cultivation?

See Also   For more information on sorting and filtering lists, see the section "Viewing the Item List" in Chapter 4, "Managing Products and Services."

Job Types and Quotes

In Chapter 6, "Managing Jobs," you learned how to set up job details in Small Business Accounting and the difference between a fixed fee job and a time and materials job. You can specify the details of a fixed fee or time and materials job by assigning it to a quote. You can then use the Job Estimates vs. Actuals Detail or Job Estimates vs. Actuals Summary report to compare the quote with the actual figures before and after the job is completed. For a fixed fee job, a quote can include line item details, but many small businesses include only one line item for the entire job (for the amount of the fixed fee). For a time and materials job, the quote should list the estimated cost and markup of each item. For more information about reports, see Chapter 14, "Creating Reports to Manage Your Business."

Managing Accepted and Rejected Quotes

A quote that you prepare is not a posted transaction. In other words, a quote itself does not become part of your accounting records in the way that a journal entry or an invoice does. However, each quote that you submit to a customer, whether through e-mail, regular mail, or in person, needs to be tracked so that you know when the status of a quote changes and can then take the action required.

A quote that a customer accepts can be converted to an invoice or a sales order so that the transaction becomes an entry in your accounting records. If a customer does not accept a quote, you should change the status of the quote to **Rejected** and enter a brief memo on the quote form to indicate why the customer didn't accept the quote. You can also edit a quote that a customer rejects and create a new open quote that you present to the customer again. Finally, you can delete a quote that you no longer need for your company's records. For example, you can delete a quote that passes its expiration date without the customer accepting or rejecting the quote.

You might have no other work to do on a quote that has been rejected. The sales opportunity that the quote represents falls through, and you change the status of the quote to **Rejected** to keep a record of your business activity. However, a customer might reject a quote, give you feedback about why the quote is not acceptable, and give you the opportunity to change the pricing or other terms of the quote so that it better meets the customer's needs.

When you edit a rejected quote, the status of the quote changes to **Open**. You can then make changes to the list of products and services, discounts, markup, or other terms of the quote and submit the quote to the customer again.

Tip Editing a rejected quote changes the quote's status and removes the quote from the list of rejected quotes. If you want to edit the quote and keep a copy of the rejected quote so that you have a full record of your business's activity, open the quote, click **Copy and Edit** on the **File** menu, and then click **Edit** on the toolbar.

When a customer accepts a quote, you don't directly change the status of the quote to **Accepted**. Instead, you convert the quote to an invoice or a sales order. The act of converting a quote changes the quote's status and creates the new accounting document that is posted to your company's records.

You can convert a quote to an invoice or a sales order only once. A quote that pertains to a job, however, can be converted to a series of progress invoices, which each cover a portion of the work defined by the job. A sales order derived from an accepted quote acts as an agreement between your business and the customer. An invoice (or a progress invoice) relates to work already accomplished or goods delivered to the customer. A sales order can be converted to an invoice at a future date. It is used for back orders of merchandise or as a work order for services.

See Also For more information about creating and working with sales orders, see Chapter 8, "Handling Sales." For more information about working with invoices, see Chapter 9, "Managing Invoices."

In this exercise, you will work with the list of quotes in the Fabrikam sample company to learn about the different actions you take to manage a quote after a customer accepts or rejects the quote.

OPEN the Fabrikam sample file if you have closed it.

1 In the **Navigation** Pane, click **Customers**.

The **Customers** home page appears.

2 Under **Find**, click **Quotes**.

The **Quote List** appears.

3 If necessary, click the **Current View** down arrow and then click **Open**.

The **Quote List** displays only open quotes.

4 In the **Quote List**, double-click quote **1037**, for the customer Sean Purcell.

The quote for Sean Purcell appears in a quote form.

5 In the **Memo** box, type Rejected because prices are too high.

6 On the **Actions** menu, click **Reject Quote**.

7 On the toolbar, click **Save and Close**.

8 In the **Current View** list, click **Rejected**.

The **Quote List** displays only those quotes that have been rejected.

9 In the list of rejected quotes, double-click quote **1037** for Sean Purcell.

The quote for Sean Purcell appears in a quote form.

10 On the toolbar, click **Edit**.

The quote opens for editing.

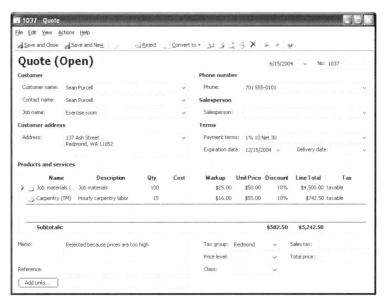

11   In the **Price level** list, click **Large Customer**.

Adding this price level to the quote applies an additional 10 percent discount to the total amount of the quote.

12   In the **Memo** field, type Additional 10 percent discount applied as more business is expected.

13   On the toolbar, click **Save and Close**.

14   In the **Current View** list, click **Open**.

The **Quote List** displays only those quotes that are open.

15   Double-click quote number **1037**, for customer Sean Purcell.

16   On the toolbar, point to **Convert To**, and then click **Invoice**.

The quote appears.

The status of the quote changes to **Accepted**, and both the quote and the invoice now appear on the **Financial History** tab of the customer record.

17   To save the invoice, on the toolbar, click **Save and Close**.

After you convert the quote, it no longer appears in the list of open quotes.

Creating a Quote Template

Small Business Accounting includes templates designed in Microsoft Office Word that you can use for presenting quotes to customers. Like templates for customer statements, invoices, and other accounting documents, the templates for quotes help keep the information you present to customers consistent. Using the same template for all of your accounting documents—and similar looking templates for other business documents—is part of your company's identity and provides a professional look and feel to your customers. The templates you use for quotes, for example, should include formatting and design elements that are like those you use in the template for a customer statement. Using templates not only enables you to maintain a consistent quality to your business documents, but it also helps you avoid the need to create and format every document you send individually.

See Also   For more information on creating XML-based Word templates, see the section "Creating a Customer Statement Template" in Chapter 5, "Setting Up Customer Information."

Key Points

- You build quotes using the products and services you've defined as items in your company records.

- Modify the discounts and product markups in a quote to balance the need to make the quote competitive with the need to realize a profit.

- You should be sure to specify an expiration date for a quote and describe conditions and assumptions you used to prepare the quote.

- A quote that a customer accepts is converted to an invoice or a sales order.

Enter a sale,
page 131

View and manipulate
the sales order list,
page 138

Edit a sale order,
page 140

Untitled -Sales Order

File Edit View Actions Help

Save and Close | Save and New | Create from | Create Invoice

Sales Order (Not Invoiced)

6/30/2005 No: 5

Customer

Customer name:
Contact name:

Billing address

Bill to:

Phone number

Phone:

Salesperson

Salesperson:

Terms

Payment terms:

Delivery date:

Products and services

Name	Unit Price	Description	Qty.	Invoiced	Line Total	Tax
	$0.00		1		$0.00	

$0.00

Tax group: None
Price level:

Sales tax:
Total price:
To be invoiced:

Northwind Traders - Microsoft Small Business Accounting

File Edit View Company Customers Vendors Employees Banking Reports Actions Help

New | Find

Company

Start a Task
- New Account
- New Journal Entry
- Forecast Cash Flow
- Pay Sales Tax

Find
- Chart of Accounts
- Journal Entries
- Items

Company
Customers
Vendors
Employees
Banking
Reports

Sales Order List

Current View: All

Date	No.	Customer Name	Phone	Delivery_	Total Pri_
Add a new Sales Order					
7/28/20...	8	Nearby Sporting Goods			$791.65
1/30/20...	6	Nearby Sporting Goods			$1,663.47
4/30/20...	3	Adventure Works			$1,735.50

Untitled -Sales Order

File Edit View Actions Help

Save and Close | Save and New | Create from | Create Invoice

Sales Order (Not Invoiced)

6/30/2005 No: 10

Customer

Customer name: Adventure Works
Contact name: Garrett Young

Billing address

Bill to: 789 3rd Street
Toronto, ON R3H 1A8

Shipping address

Ship to:

Phone number

Phone:

Salesperson

Salesperson:

Terms

Payment terms: Net 15
Shipping terms:
Shipping method: Mail
Delivery date:

Products and services

Name	Description	Qty.	Unit Price	Discount	Back Order	Invoiced	Line Total	Tax
Set with Bag	Golf Club Set with Bag	1	$1,299.99	0%			$1,299.99	taxable
Subtotals:			$0.00				$1,299.99	

Memo:
Reference:
Add Links...

Tax group: Out of State Sale
Price level:

Sales tax:
Total price:
To be invoiced:

Chapter 8 at a Glance

8 Handling Sales

In this chapter you will learn to:

✔ Enter a sale.

✔ View and manipulate the sales order list.

✔ Create sales order templates.

✔ Edit sales orders.

✔ Manage back orders.

Sales revenue forms the backbone of any business. Regardless of whether you sell products or services, you need to find customers for your wares. When someone asks to buy one of your products or an hour of your consulting time, you need to create a record of the request in Microsoft Office Small Business Accounting 2006. That record is known as a *sales order*. In this chapter, you'll learn how to create a sales order, view and manipulate the sales order list, create sales order templates, edit existing sales orders, and manage back orders (orders you can't fulfill without receiving additional products into inventory).

See Also Do you need only a quick refresher on the topics in this chapter? See the Quick Reference entries on pages xxviii–xxix.

Entering a Sales Order

A sale is a sale. It's nice to know whether you won a bidding contest or attracted the customer through word-of-mouth advertising, but the sale is the important part of the equation. In Small Business Accounting, you represent a customer's intention to buy by using a sales order. You can create a sales order for any customer with active status, although you might need to create a new customer record before you start to create your sales order.

See Also For more information on creating a new customer record, see Chapter 5, "Setting Up Customer Information."

The default sales order template depends on the type of company you set up. If you created a service-based company, the **Service** template appears. If you created a product-based company, the **Product** template appears. The **Product** and **Service** templates are similar, but the **Product** template contains a **Ship To** section, which contains information on where to deliver your product.

There are two ways you can create a new sales order: from scratch or by basing the new sales order on an existing quote.

Creating a Sales Order from Scratch

If you get a call from a customer who wants to place an order, you can open a blank sales order form.

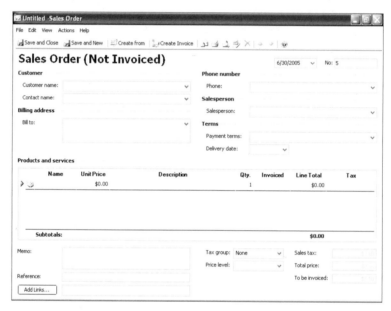

After you display the sales order form, you can fill in the data required to initiate the transaction.

In this exercise you will create a sales order from scratch.

BE SURE TO start Small Business Accounting if it is not already running.

OPEN the Fabrikam sample file.

1 On the **Customers** menu, click **Customers Home**.

The **Customers** home page appears.

2 In the **Start a Task** section of the **Customers** home page, click **New Sales Order**.

A new sales order form based on the default template appears.

3 If the sales order form contains a **Shipping Address** section (indicating that it is the **Product** template) open the **Actions** menu, point to **Select Template**, and click **Service**.

4 Click the **Customer Name** down arrow, and then click **Coho Winery**.

Contact information for Coho Winery appears in the top section of the sales order form.

5 In the **Terms** section of the form, click the **Payment Terms** down arrow and then click **1% 10 Net 30**.

6 Click the **Delivery Date** down arrow.

A calendar control appears.

7 Use the calendar control to select a delivery date of July 12, 2006.

The value **7/12/2006** appears in the **Delivery Date** field.

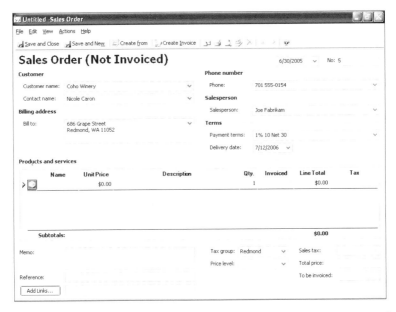

8 In the **Products and Services** section of the form, click the first **Name** field, click the down arrow that appears, and then click **Plumbing Labor (TM)**.

The new item appears in the **Products and Services** list.

9 In the **Products and Services** list, click anywhere below the list item you just created.

A new item line appears.

10 Click the new **Name** field, click the down arrow that appears, and then click **Plumbing Materials (FF)**.

The new item appears in the **Products and Services** list.

11 Right-click the **Plumbing Labor** item, and then click **Delete**.

The item disappears from the **Products and Services** list.

12 Click the **Price Level** down arrow, and then click **Preferred Customer -15%**.

The prices and sales tax displayed in the sales order change to reflect the discount.

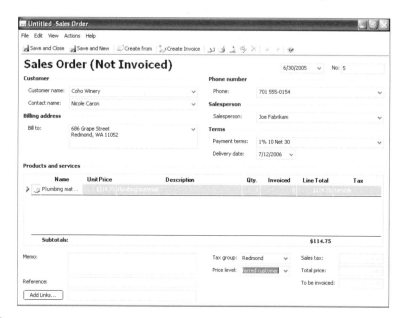

13 On the sales order form toolbar, click the **Save and Close** button.

Small Business Accounting saves your sales order and closes the sales order form.

Creating a Sales Order from a Quote

If you've already generated a quote that's been accepted by a customer, you can base your sales order on the contents of that quote. All you need to do is use the controls on the **Customers** home page to start a new sales order and then select the quote on which you want to base your sales order.

Caution   The Fabrikam sample company file doesn't contain any open quotes you can use to create a sales order, but you will have created a quote if you performed all of the exercises in Chapter 7, "Generating and Managing Quotes." If you did create a quote as you worked through that chapter, use it in this exercise. If you haven't created a quote yet, please go back to Chapter 7 and follow the directions in the exercise in the section named "Creating a Quote."

In this exercise you will create a sales order from a quote.

OPEN the Fabrikam sample file if you have closed it.

1 On the **Customers** menu, click **Customers Home**.

The **Customers** home page appears.

2 In the **Start a Task** section of the **Customers** home page, click **New Sales Order**.

A new sales order based on the default template appears.

3 On the toolbar, click the **Create From** button.

The **Select a Quote** dialog box appears.

4 Click the quote for **City Power and Light**.

5 Click **OK**.

The **Select a Quote** dialog box disappears and the sales order form appears, now containing the customer and item information from the quote.

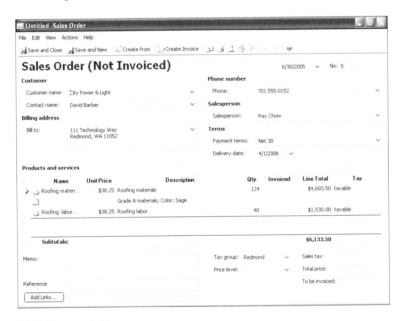

6 Click **Save and Close**.

Small Business Accounting saves your sales order and closes the sales order form.

Customizing Sales Order Forms

One of the joys of owning your own business is that you have the power to make decisions, choose your company's products, and decide how everything looks. The bad news is that you actually have to make all of those decisions, or have someone make them for you. It's a lot of work, but it's important that everything be exactly the way you want it to be. One of the ways you can customize your company's presence is by changing the appearance of Small Business Accounting sales orders.

Note   Customizing a sales order form doesn't change how Small Business Accounting exports or prints your data.

One thing you can't change is the information in the top section of a sales order. Small Business Accounting needs that information to manage the sale within your database, and you need that information on display in case you need to be reminded about your customer's contact details or the promised delivery date. If you like, you can change the columns displayed in the **Products and Services** list at the bottom of your sales orders.

To change the columns that appear in the **Products and Services** list, open the **View** menu and click **Add/Remove Columns**. The **Grid Customization** dialog box appears.

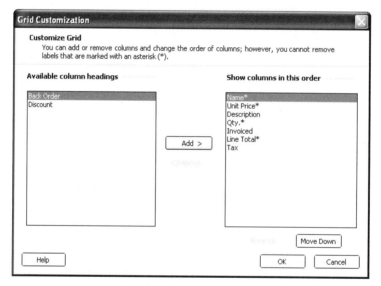

Small Business Accounting displays columns that appear in the **Show Columns in This Order** list; columns in the **Available Column Headings** list are hidden. You can add a column from the **Available Column Headings** list to your sales order by clicking the column name and then clicking the **Add** button. Similarly, you can remove a column from the **Products and Services** list by clicking the column name in the **Show Columns in This Order** list and then clicking the **Remove** button. Be aware, though, that you can't remove any column with an asterisk next to its name, such as **Name**, **Quantity**, **Unit Price**, and **Line Total**.

Note   When you add a column, it appears at the bottom of the **Show Columns in This Order** list, regardless of the active column names in that list.

You can also use the **Grid Customization** dialog box to change the order in which the fields appear in the **Products and Services** list. For example, you might prefer to display the **Unit Price** column to the left of the **Qty.** (quantity) instead of to the right, as in the **Products and Services** list default configuration. To change the order in which the columns appear, open the **View** menu and then click **Add/Remove Columns** to display the **Grid Customization** dialog box. Click the name of the column you want to reposition and then either click the **Move Up** button to move the column up in the **Show Columns in This Order** list (to the left in the **Products and Services** list), or click the column's name and then click the **Move Down** button to move the column down in the **Show Columns in This Order** list (to the right in the **Products and Services** list).

In the following exercise, you will customize the appearance of your sales order form.

OPEN the Fabrikam sample file if you have closed it.

1 On the **Customers** menu, point to **Customer Lists** and then click **Sales Orders**.

The **Sales Order List** appears.

2 In the **Sales Orders List**, double-click the **Coho Winery** sale with a delivery date of July 12, 2006.

The Coho Winery sales order appears.

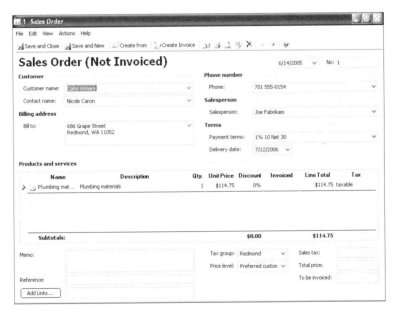

3 On the **View** menu, click **Add/Remove Columns**.

The **Grid Customization** dialog box appears.

4 In the **Show Columns in This Order** list, click the **Discount** column.

5   Click the **Remove** button.

The **Discount** column moves to the **Available Column Headings** list.

6   In the **Show Columns in This Order** list, click the **Unit Price** column.

7   Click the **Move Up** button.

The **Unit Price** column heading moves above the **Qty.** heading in the **Show Columns in This Order** list.

8   **Click OK**.

The **Unit Price** column moves to the left of the **Qty.** column in the **Products and Services** list, and the **Discount** column has been removed.

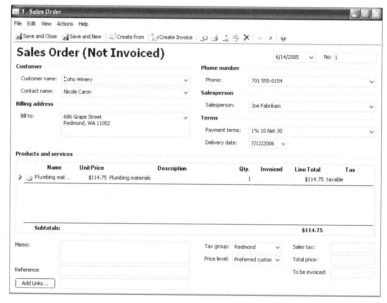

9   Click **Save and Close**.

Small Business Accounting saves your sales order and closes the sales order form.

Viewing and Manipulating the Sales Order List

Small Business Accounting stores all of your sales orders in a single list, the sales order list. To display the sales order list, open the **Customers** menu, point to **Customer Lists**, and then click **Sales Orders**. The **Sales Order List** from the sample Northwind Traders database shows three sales orders.

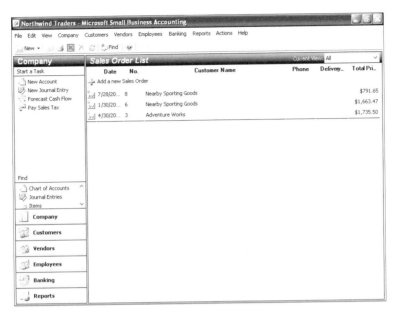

Manipulating the Sales Order List

If you've been in business for a while, it's very likely that your sales order list is fairly long. You can rearrange and limit the data that appears in your sales order list by using the list manipulation techniques covered in the section "Viewing the Item List" in Chapter 4, "Managing Products and Services."

Creating Sales Order Templates

Small Business Accounting templates use the *Extensible Markup Language (XML)* to encode their data. XML is a standard that enables you to record metadata (data about your data) in the same document as the original data. In Small Business Accounting templates, for example, you could have XML codes, called tags, which delineate customer names, their shipping address, and so on. When you create a template in Microsoft Office Word, Word lists the data elements such as customer data that you can include in your sales order in the **Document Actions** pane, at the right edge of the Word program window.

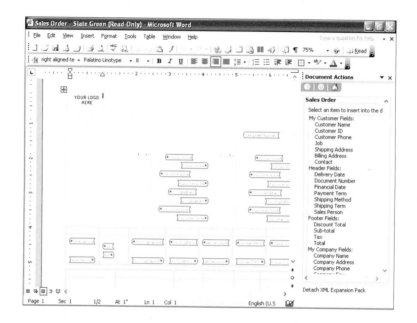

See Also For more information on creating XML-based Word templates, see the section "Creating a Customer Statement Template" in Chapter 5, "Setting Up Customer Information."

Editing Sales Orders

You try to keep the mistakes in your business to a minimum, but they always seem to crop up at the worst times. If you run a small business, the person taking phone orders is often performing another task at the same time, such as answering other phone calls, minding a retail counter, or checking stock. Or, if you're the person taking the orders, you might be busy running the business. In other words, it's very easy to make mistakes when you enter sales orders.

Fortunately, you can edit a sales order as long as one of two conditions exists:

■   You have not created an invoice based on the sales order.

■   You have only created a partial invoice based on the sales order.

If you've created a full invoice based on a sales order, you will need to delete the existing invoice, delete the existing sales order, and then create a new sales order.

When you display the **Sales Order List** and double-click a sales order, the sales order appears in an editable window. From there, you can change any of the information in the sales order and use it to generate a new invoice.

In this exercise, you will edit the Coho Winery sales order to change the number of hours of plumbing labor requested and to choose a new delivery date.

OPEN the Fabrikam sample file.

1 On the **Customers** menu, point to **Customer Lists,** and then click **Sales Orders.**

The **Sales Order List** appears.

2 Double-click the **Coho Winery** order.

The Coho Winery order appears in a new sales order form.

3 In the **Terms** section of the sales order window, click in the **Delivery Date** field and edit the date so that it reads **7/14/2006**.

4 In the **Products and Services** list, click in the **Qty.** field on the first row of the **Products and Services** list.

5 Type 2.

6 Click **Save and Close**.

Small Business Accounting saves your changes and closes the sales order.

Managing Back Orders

When you sell a popular product, you benefit from the profits the sales generate. Unfortunately, you also risk running out of that popular product. Small hardware stores are particularly vulnerable to this phenomenon if they stock an item featured at a home improvement show. When you have only a few units of a suddenly desirable doorknob in stock but anticipate being able to get more units from your supplier, you might need to accept orders from your customers and ship their doorknobs when they arrive. The items you don't have in stock are said to be on *back order*.

The procedure to handle back orders combines the capabilities of sales orders and invoices. Whenever you create a sales order that includes items that must be back ordered, the quantity of items not in stock appears in the **Back Order** column of the **Products and Services** list.

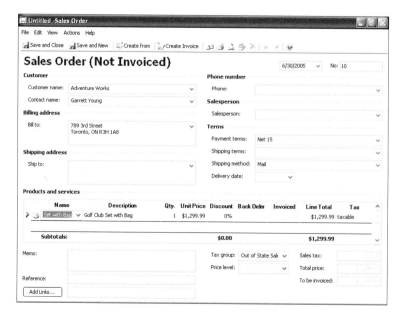

Your next steps are to create a partial invoice that charges the customer for only those items you have in stock, order the items you need, receive the items into inventory, create an invoice for the remaining items, and then ship the order with the invoice.

See Also   For more information on creating a partial invoice, see Chapter 9, "Preparing and Managing Invoices." For more information on ordering and receiving items into inventory, see Chapter 11, "Purchasing from and Paying Vendors."

You can choose to have Small Business Accounting remind you of your back orders on the **Company** home page. In this exercise you will turn on this reminder.

OPEN the Fabrikam sample file.

1   If necessary, in the **Navigation** pane, click **Company**.

     The **Company** home page appears.

2   At the bottom right corner of the **Today's Reminders** section, click the **Add/Remove** button.

     The **Add/Remove Reminders** dialog box appears.

3   Select the **Back Orders** check box.

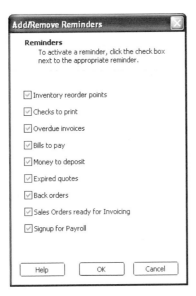

4 Click **OK**.

The **Add/Remove Reminders** dialog box disappears. Small Business Accounting will now inform you when there are items on back order.

Key Points

- You can enter sales orders quickly by using sales order forms.

- Rather than re-type information from a quote, create a sales order based on that quote.

- Customize the sales order form so that the fields appear in the order you want.

- You can create Word templates that enable you to print customized sales orders.

- Be sure to have Small Business Accounting remind you of any items on back order.

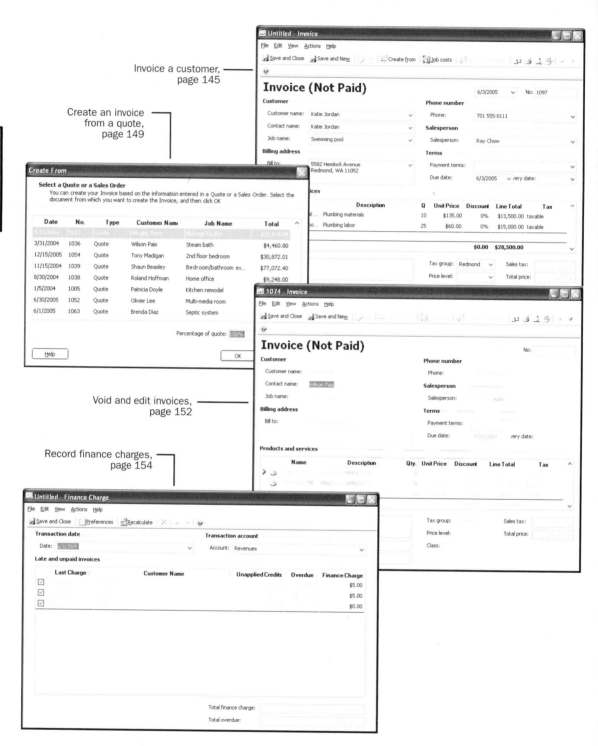

Invoice a customer,
page 145

Create an invoice
from a quote,
page 149

Void and edit invoices,
page 152

Record finance charges,
page 154

Chapter 9 at a Glance

9 Preparing and Managing Invoices

In this chapter you will learn to:

✔ Invoice a customer.

✔ Create an invoice from a quote or a job.

✔ Void and edit invoices.

✔ Record a finance charge.

An invoice shows the products and services that a customer has purchased, the quantity of each item, the amount of the sale, the date the invoice is due, payment terms, and other details of a sales transaction. The items billed on an invoice can include materials from your inventory, professional services or labor that you provide, or expenses incurred that you pass on to the customer.

Microsoft Office Small Business Accounting 2006 provides several ways to create invoices. You can create an invoice from scratch by filling in the invoice form with customer information and the list of products and services you are billing for. You can also create an invoice from a quote (or a sales order) that you have provided to a customer or, if your company is set up to use jobs, create an invoice from a job record. For invoices related to jobs, you can create a progress invoice that bills the customer for a percentage of the job amount or itemize the time, expenses, and materials that are associated with the job in Small Business Accounting.

In this chapter, you'll learn about the steps you take to create and work with invoices. You'll learn about the different ways to create an invoice. You'll also learn how to handle finance charges for past due invoices, and how to void and edit an invoice.

See Also Do you need only a quick refresher on the topics in this chapter? See the Quick Reference entries on pages xxix–xxxi.

Invoicing a Customer

An *invoice* is a request for payment you send to a customer. Your invoices contain customer information, a list of products and services you are billing for, and the quantities, prices, discounts, and other details that are part of the sale. When you save an invoice, Small Business Accounting posts it to your company's accounts, and it becomes a permanent part of your records.

Important   You cannot delete an invoice once it is posted. The act of posting the invoice generates *journal entries* that debit (increase) the amount of your accounts receivable and credit other accounts such as labor costs or inventory. You can void an invoice if the invoice is no longer valid or edit an invoice to change or update its details or terms. For information about how to void an invoice, see the section "Voiding and Editing an Invoice" later in this chapter.

To create an invoice, open the **Customers** menu, point to **New**, and then click **New Invoice** to display a blank invoice form.

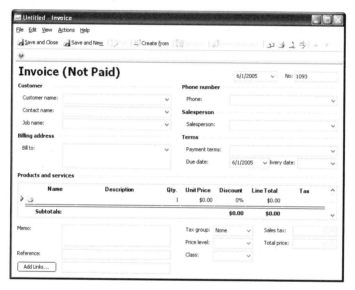

When you create an invoice, the status of the invoice is **Not Paid**. Small Business Accounting fills in the current date and assigns a number to the invoice, but you can change the invoice number to conform to your company's numbering system.

You use the top portion of the invoice form to enter customer information, payment terms, the due date for the invoice, and the delivery date. In the **Products and Services** area of the invoice form, you list the items the invoice covers. Each line item in an invoice shows the name and a description of the item, the quantity, unit price, discount, the line total, and the tax status of the item.

If you assigned a customer to a tax group, you can find that information at the bottom of the form. The sales tax rates defined in the tax codes that are included in the tax group are applied to the price of items as you build the invoice.

See Also   For information about creating customer records and about defining tax groups and tax codes, see Chapter 5, "Setting Up Customer Information."

Note   If you select the **Use Job** option in the **Company Preferences** dialog box, the invoice form includes the **Job Name** field. Later in this chapter, you'll learn more about creating invoices for jobs. If you select the **Use Class** option as a company preference, the invoice form includes the **Class** field. You can use this field to specify which class a quote belongs to. For example, if you have set up sales regions as classes, you can designate the region in the invoice.

The list of products and services are those you have set up as items. The description of the item comes from the item record. As part of creating an invoice, you can add an item to the list by clicking **Add a New Item**. Also, if you type a name of an item that is not included in the item list, Small Business Accounting requires that you create a record for the item before you continue creating the invoice.

A line item in an invoice can also refer to an account in a company's chart of accounts, specify a sales tax that applies to the quote, or provide a comment on a line item or another aspect of the quote. To change the type of line item, click the icon in the first cell of the line item row and then select the type of line item you want to use: **Item**, **Comment**, **Sales Tax**, or **Account**.

Tip   To apply a discount to the total amount of the quote rather than to a single line item, add an **Account** line item to the quote, specify the Discount expense account, and then enter the amount of the discount in the **Unit Price** field.

In this exercise, you'll create an invoice from scratch by filling in the fields in the invoice form. (In the exercise that follows, you'll create an invoice from a quote.)

BE SURE TO start Small Business Accounting if it is not already running.

OPEN the Fabrikam sample file.

1   On the **Customers** menu, point to **New**, and then click **New Invoice**.

A blank invoice form appears.

2   Click the **Customer Name** down arrow, and then click **Brenda Diaz**.

The appropriate customer information appears in the invoice.

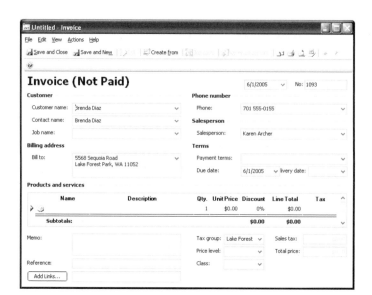

3 In the **Payment terms** field, click **Net 30**.

The due date changes to reflect the time period of the payment term.

4 In the **Delivery Date** field, type a date later than the present date.

5 Under **Products and Services**, click in the **Name** column for the first row, click the down arrow, and then click **Carpentry (TM)** from the list of product or services.

The **Carpentry (TM)** item appears in the **Products and Services** grid.

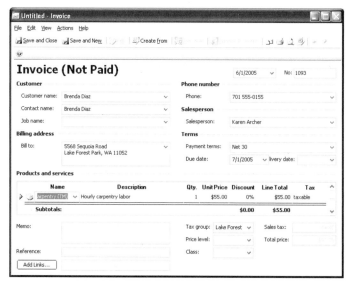

6 Click in the leftmost column of the second row, and then click **Comment**.

7   In the **Description** field, type Framed addition to bedroom.

8   In the line item for hourly carpentry labor, in the **Qty.** (Quantity) field, type 24.

9   In the **Discount** field, type 5.

10   In the row below the comment you entered in step 7, click in the **Name** column and then select **Framing/finish materials** from the item list.

11   In the **Qty.** field, type 40.

12   In the **Price level** list, click **Preferred Customer**.

See Also   For information about defining price levels and assigning a price level to a customer, see Chapter 5, "Setting Up Customer Information."

---

13   Click the **Save and Close** button on the toolbar.

Small Business Accounting saves your invoice, and the invoice form disappears.

Creating an Invoice from a Quote or a Job

In Chapter 7, "Generating and Managing Quotes," you learned that you can convert a quote (or a sales order) to an invoice. Similarly, you can create an invoice from a quote by clicking **Create from** on the invoice form toolbar.

A quote that details the products and services for a job that you have set up in Small Business Accounting can serve as the basis of a *progress invoice* in which you bill for a specified percentage of a job. You can also itemize job costs on an invoice you create from a quote.

The value that you enter in the **Percentage of Quote** box in the **Create From** dialog box reflects the percentage of the costs specified on the quote that you want to bill for on this invoice. If you are billing the entire amount of the quote, the percentage should be 100.

The invoice form includes a comment in the **Products and Services** area that indicates the percentage being billed. You can add another comment to this invoice to provide details to the customer about the progress of the work or add other line items to bill for miscellaneous expenses not covered by the quote.

You can use the **Time and Materials** dialog box to compile an itemized job invoice. The entries on the **Items** tab originate from a quote that is associated with a job. Entries on the **Time** tab are created when an employee bills time to a specific job. Entries on the **Expense** tab are created when you record vendor expenses that relate to a job.

See Also For more information about billing employee time, see Chapter 12, "Managing Employee Time and Payroll." For more information about vendor expenses, see Chapter 11, "Purchasing from and Paying Vendors."

In addition to generating an invoice from the **Customers** home page, you can use the job list to create an invoice for a particular job. You can use this approach to create a progress invoice for a fixed fee job or an itemized invoice for a time and materials job.

See Also For more information about fixed fee and time and material jobs, see Chapter 6, "Managing Jobs."

Note To set up jobs in Small Business Accounting, you must select the option **Use Jobs** in the **Company Preferences** dialog box.

In this exercise, you will use quotes from the Fabrikam sample company to create a progress invoice from a quote and add detailed job costs to an invoice.

OPEN the Fabrikam sample file if you have closed it.

1 On the Customers menu, point to New, and then click New Invoice.

A blank invoice form appears.

2 On the invoice form toolbar, click Create from.

The **Create From** dialog box appears.

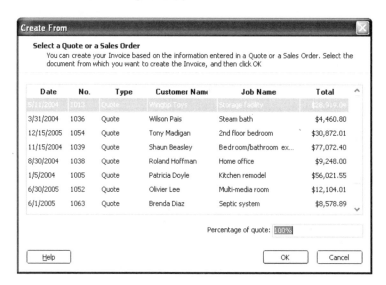

3 Click quote number **1038** for customer **Roland Hoffman**.

Tip For a long list of quotes and sales orders, you can click a column heading to sort the list by date, customer name, or job name, for example.

4 In the **Percentage of Quote** box, type 50.

5 Click **OK**.

The **Create From** dialog box disappears.

6 On the invoice form toolbar, click **Save and Close**.

The invoice disappears.

7 On the **Navigation** pane, under **Find**, click **Jobs**.

The **Job List** appears.

8 In the **Job List**, click the job named **Swimming pool** for customer **Katie Jordan**.

9 On the **Actions** menu, click **New Invoice for Job**.

An invoice form appears.

10 On the invoice form toolbar, click **Job Costs**.

The **Time and Materials** dialog box appears.

11 Click the **Items** tab.

The **Items** tab appears.

12 Clear the check boxes for **Foundation/Masonry Materials** and **Foundation/ Masonry Labor**, and select the **Plumbing Materials** and **Plumbing Labor (FF)** check boxes.

13 Click **OK**.

The new invoice appears.

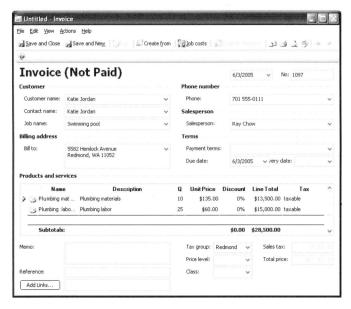

14 Click **Save and Close**.

Small Business Accounting saves the invoice.

Sales Orders and Partial Invoices

Like a quote, a sales order can be used as the basis of an invoice in Small Business Accounting. Creating an invoice from a sales order lets you bill a customer for the entire order, or you can create a partial invoice for cases when some of the items the customer has ordered must be back ordered or provided at a later date.

You create a partial invoice by adjusting the values in the **Qty.** field on the invoice form. For example, you have a sales order for 10 items and can deliver and bill for 6 of those items. When you first create an invoice from the sales order, you change the **Qty.** field from 10 to 6, and Small Business Accounting calculates the amount of the invoice based on 6 units. When you create another invoice from the sales order, the **Qty.** field will show that only 4 items remain.

Voiding and Editing Invoices

When you save an invoice, the invoice is posted to your company's books. You cannot delete an invoice that has been posted, but you can make changes to the invoice or void an invoice that is no longer valid. After you void an invoice, you cannot change the status of the invoice to open again. If you want to charge your customer for the items listed in the voided invoice, you must create a new invoice.

You can use a voided invoice as the basis for a new invoice. For example, if you need to change the discount terms on an invoice, you can void the invoice and then make a copy of the voided invoice to edit. If you sell the same items to the same customer or want to create an invoice that is similar to an existing one, you can create a new invoice by copying an invoice and editing the copy.

When you void an invoice, Small Business Accounting enters a reverse posting with the same date as the original invoice so that the invoice does not appear in your general ledger but a record of the transaction is retained.

Note   When you void an invoice, the label VOID appears on the invoice form. However, the label does not appear when you send a voided invoice as an e-mail message. To avoid confusion about the status of the invoice, you can attach the voided invoice to the e-mail message instead.

In this exercise, you will void an invoice and edit an invoice using examples from Fabrikam, Inc.

OPEN the Fabrikam sample file if you have closed it.

1   In the **Navigation** pane, click **Customers**.

2   Under **Find**, click **Invoices**.

3   In the invoice list, double-click invoice number **1074**, for the customer **Wilson Pais**.

4   On the **Actions** menu, click **Void**, and then click **Yes** in the message box.

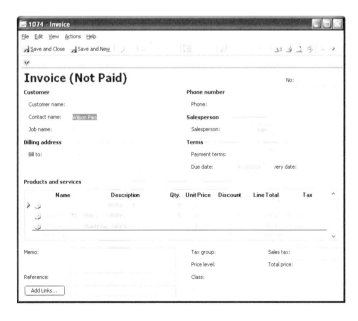

> **Tip** Use the **Memo** box on the invoice form to enter a brief description for the reason this invoice is no longer valid. To open voided invoices, select **Voided** from the **Current View** list, and then double-click the invoice.

5 On the toolbar, click **Save and Close**.

6 In the **Current View** box at the top right of the invoice list, click **Voided**.

7 In the list of voided invoices, double-click invoice **1074**.

8 On the **File** menu, click **Copy and Edit**.

The new invoice appears with the customer information and line items from the original. Small Business Accounting assigns a new number to the invoice and sets the date to the current date. You can now make changes to the details of the invoice. The status of the voided invoice that you used as the basis of the new invoice does not change. The voided invoice is retained in your accounting records.

See Also For more information on sorting and filtering lists, see the section named "Viewing the Item List" in Chapter 4, "Managing Products and Services."

Recording a Finance Charge

Among the company preferences you can set is the finance charge for unpaid balances on past due invoices. To calculate a finance charge, you specify a default value for the annual interest rate at which the finance charge is assessed, a default minimum charge, the number of grace days, and whether the finance charge is calculated from the invoice due date or the date of the invoice itself.

Each finance charge that is assessed is included in the invoice list. The amount of a finance charge is calculated on the unpaid balance for all open invoices. You should apply any payments and credits to overdue invoices before you apply a finance charge.

In this exercise, you'll review the settings for finance charges in the **Company Preferences** dialog box and then apply a finance charge to a customer balance.

OPEN the Fabrikam sample file if you have closed it.

1 In the **Navigation** pane, click **Customers**.

2 Under **Start a Task**, click **Finance Charge**.

The **Finance Charge** form appears.

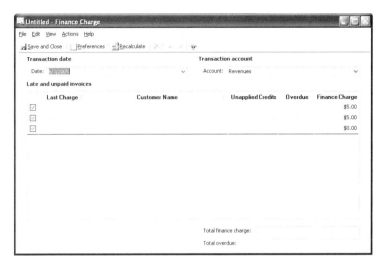

3 Clear the check boxes on the rows for the **John Kane** and **Wilson Pais** accounts.

4 In the **Finance Charge** column of the row that contains Katie Jordan's overdue invoice, type 25.

> **Tip** You can change the amount assessed for finance charges by clicking **Preferences** on the toolbar and then changing the settings on the **Customer** tab of the **Company Preferences** dialog box.

5 On the toolbar, click **Save and Close**.

The **Finance Charge** form disappears.

Designing an Invoice Template

Small Business Accounting includes templates designed in Microsoft Office Word that you can use to format invoices you send to customers. Like templates for customer statements, quotes, and other accounting documents, the templates for invoices help keep the information you present to customers consistent.

An invoice template displays your company's name and address, the customer's contact information, and the product and financial details that the invoice applies to. You can add or remove fields, design the layout of the template, and apply Word formatting to specify fonts and other elements you want to use on the template.

The invoice templates (and other templates) that come with Small Business Accounting are set up as tables in Word. A table helps keep fields aligned and positioned in the document. You can adjust the width of the columns and rows in the table to match the amount of text a particular table cell needs to contain.

See Also For more information on creating XML-based Word templates, see the section "Creating a Customer Statement Template" in Chapter 5, "Setting Up Customer Information."

Key Points

- You can create invoices on their own or by using information in a quote, sales order, or job.

- Invoices are posted to your company's accounts. Once an invoice is posted, you cannot delete the invoice, but you can void or edit an invoice.

- The details of a finance charge that you can apply to an overdue invoice are set up in the **Company Preferences** dialog box.

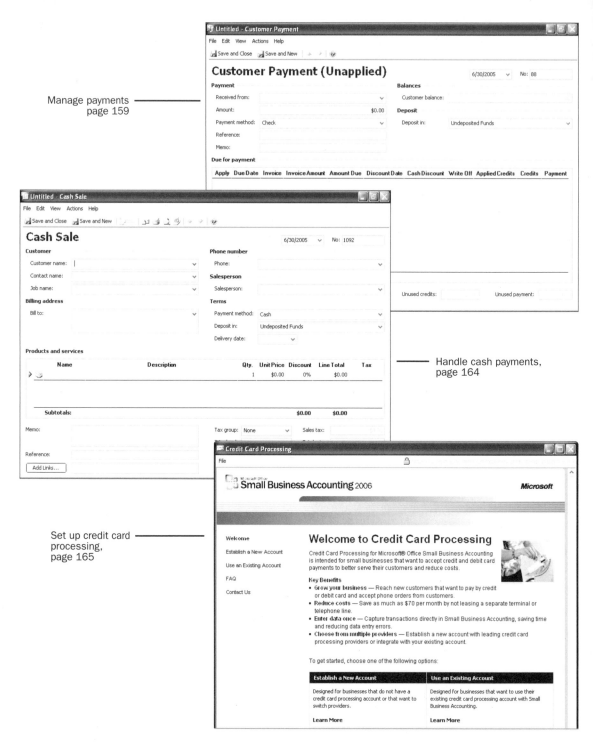

Manage payments
page 159

Handle cash payments,
page 164

Set up credit card
processing,
page 165

10 Handling Customer Payments

Without income, your company would wither on the vine. But if you don't handle your customers' payments effectively, you won't know how much money you have or who owes you what amount. Microsoft Office Small Business Accounting 2006 uses a set of consistently designed forms that enable you to track your payments, assign payments to invoices, and even handle customer returns and refunds efficiently.

In this chapter, you will learn how to manage customer payments, handle cash payments, manage refunds, and design custom credit memo templates.

See Also   Do you need only a quick refresher on the topics in this chapter? See the Quick Reference entries on pages xxxi–xxxii.

Managing Payments

You can extend credit to your customers, delivering their goods and services along with an invoice, but eventually you must get paid for your efforts. Managing your payments in Small Business Accounting means that you can be prepared for payment by check, cash, and credit card. You can also be prepared for those unfortunate times when a payment must be reversed, whether that's because a customer's check doesn't clear or there was a problem with a credit card.

Receiving Payments into Small Business Accounting

When a customer hands you a check, cash, or credit card in payment for goods or services, you can enter that payment into Small Business Accounting by using a **Customer Payment** form.

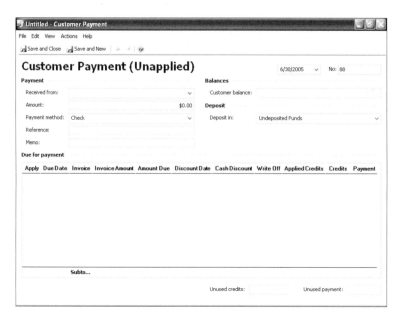

A **Customer Payment** form is very similar to other Small Business Accounting forms. It contains fields for the customer's name, the amount received, how the customer paid, the customer's remaining balance (if any) and the customer's outstanding invoices. If there is more than one outstanding item in the **Due for Payment** list, you can decide to which of the items you want to apply the payment.

Note If a customer has more than one outstanding invoice, Small Business Accounting assigns the payment to the oldest invoice by default.

In this exercise you will receive a payment into Small Business Accounting.

BE SURE TO start Small Business Accounting if it is not already running.

OPEN the Fabrikam sample file.

1 On the **Customers** menu, click **Receive Payment**.

A **Customer Payment** form appears.

2 In the unnamed date field at the top right corner of the **Customer Payment** form, type 12/3/2005.

3 Click the **Received from** down arrow, and then click **Wingtip Toys**.

The payments due from **Wingtip Toys** appear in the **Due for Payment** list.

4 In the **Amount** field, type 86895.38, and press ⌨Tab.

Small Business Accounting applies the payment amount to invoice number **1065** in the **Due for Payment** list and selects that row's **Apply** check box.

5   Click the **Deposit in** down arrow, and then click **Checking**.

6   Click **Save and New**.

Small Business Accounting saves the payment and opens a new **Customer Payment** form.

7   Click the **Received from** down arrow, and then click **Katie Jordan**.

The payments due from **Katie Jordan** appear in the **Due for Payment** list.

8   In the **Amount** field, type 100, and press Tab.

Small Business Accounting applies the payment amount to invoice number **1079** in the **Due for Payment** list and selects that row's **Apply** check box.

9   Click the **Deposit in** down arrow and then click **Checking**.

10   Click **Save and Close**.

Small Business Accounting saves the payment and closes the **Customer Payment** form.

Adding a Finance Charge

If a customer is unable to pay the entire amount due for a purchase, you have the option to charge interest on what is essentially a loan. Small Business Accounting calculates a finance charge based on the default annual interest rate you've defined on the **Customers** tab of the **Company Preferences** dialog box.

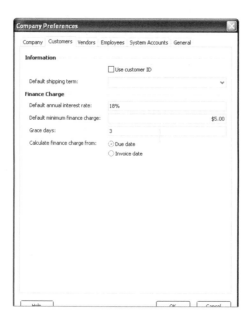

See Also For more information on setting your company preferences, see Chapter 2, "Setting Up a New Company."

When you open the **Customers** menu and click **Finance Charge**, an untitled **Finance Charge** form appears.

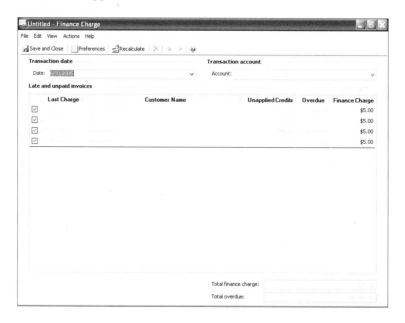

Small Business Accounting assigns a finance charge for each open invoice by default, although you can clear the check box next to any open invoices so the program won't add the finance charge to a customer's outstanding balance.

In this exercise, you will assign finance charges to selected Fabrikam customers with outstanding invoices.

OPEN the Fabrikam sample file if you have closed it.

1   On the **Customers** menu, choose **Finance Charge**.

The **Finance Charge** form appears.

2   Clear the check box next to **Wilson Pais**.

Clearing the check box tells Small Business Accounting not to assign a finance charge to customer Wilson Pais.

3   Click **Save and Close**.

Small Business Accounting assigns a finance charge to the selected customers with outstanding invoices.

Voiding a Payment

It's unfortunate, but there will be times when a customer's check is returned for insufficient funds or you run into a problem with the credit card the customer used. One possibility? It wasn't their card. When you run into these difficulties, you'll have to correct your accounts to reflect the change. You can't delete payments; they generate accounting records that the program must maintain. You can, however, void a payment so that the monies you thought you had received are removed from your account.

Voiding a payment is a straightforward process. You need to display the payment, open the **Actions** menu, click **Void**, and confirm that you want to void the payment. The original record remains in your company file, but the transaction is correctly identified as being void.

In this exercise you will void a payment.

OPEN the Fabrikam sample file if you have closed it.

1   On the **Customers** menu, point to **Customer Lists,** and then click **Payments**.

The **Payment List** appears.

2   Click the payment from **Wingtip Toys** for $86,895.38.

3   On the **Actions** menu, click **Void**.

A dialog box appears asking if you're sure you want to void the transaction.

4   Click **Yes**.

Small Business Accounting voids the payment and changes the payment's indicator to reflect its status.

Tip To prevent Small Business Accounting from displaying the verification dialog box in the future, select the **In the Future, Do Not Show this Warning** check box.

Handling Cash Sales

Many customers prefer to pay with credit or debit cards, but if you run a retail store, you must be ready to accept cash payments. Counting and securing cash can be a pain, but recording cash sales in Small Business Accounting follows procedures that are similar to those for other payment forms.

Important Some customers who pay cash do so to protect their privacy by not giving their name and contact information to the seller. You should strongly consider creating a dummy account, perhaps named *Cash Customer*, with which to associate sales to customers who don't want to release their personally identifiable information.

When a customer pays for an item by using cash, you can record the sale by opening the **Customers** menu, pointing to **New**, and then clicking **New Cash Sale**. The form that appears has fields to enter the customer's name (if they wish to share it), the delivery date, and the products and services purchased. When you're done entering the transaction, you can either click **Save and Close** to conclude entering sales, or click **Save and New** to open a blank **Cash Sale** form.

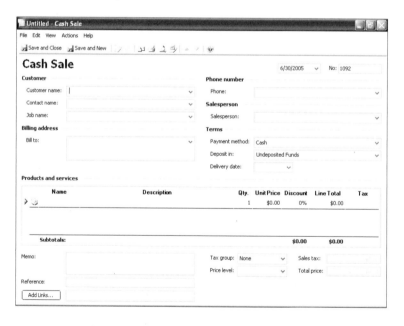

Note Because cash sales generate accounting records, you can't delete cash sales from your company file. To change a cash sale's record, you need to void or edit the transaction. The procedure to void a transaction appears earlier in this chapter.

In this exercise, you will record a cash sale in Small Business Accounting.

OPEN the Fabrikam sample file if you have closed it.

1   On the **Customers** menu, point to **New**, and then click **New Cash Sale**.

A blank **Cash Sale** form appears.

2   Click the **Customer Name** down arrow and then click **Katie Jordan**.

3   On the first line of the **Products and Services** list, click in the **Name** field.

4   Click the down arrow that appears and then click **Electrical Materials (FF)**.

5   Click **Save and Close**.

Small Business Accounting records the cash sale.

Setting Up Credit Card Processing

Cash might still be the backbone of modern commerce, but credit cards make transactions much easier to handle. You can accumulate sales information electronically, you don't have to count a stack of dirty paper, and there's no need for one or two daily trips to the bank. You record credit card payments by using the procedures for receiving payment described earlier in this chapter. If you're already set up with a credit card merchant account, you can enter that information into Small Business Accounting. If you don't have a merchant account, you can sign up for one from within the program.

Note   Credit card processing plan details were still being finalized as this book went to press.

In this exercise, you will display the Manage Credit Card Processing Wizard and set up your credit card processing account.

Important   You can't sign up for credit card processing from the Fabrikam or Northwind Traders sample company files. To sign up for credit card processing, create a file for your small business.

1   On the **Customers** menu, point to **Credit Card Processing** and then click **Sign Up for Credit Card Processing**.

The Credit Card Processing Wizard appears.

2   Under **Establish a New Account**, click the **Learn More** link.

The **Establish a New Account** wizard page, which contains a list of plans from which to choose, appears.

3   Click the plan to which you want to subscribe and follow the directions in the wizard to sign up.

Managing Returns and Refunds

It makes good business sense to allow your customers to return items they have purchased. Sometimes customers leave your store with products that need to be fixed or replaced. In some cases, your customer might have bought a product for a project that didn't materialize, purchased too many units of a product, or simply had a change of mind about a purchase. As a courtesy (or as a matter of law in some jurisdictions), you should accept the return of the unwanted product, provided the customer returns the item within a reasonable time and in a condition that allows the item to be re-sold.

The basic mechanism for customer refunds is the credit memo, which you can create by opening the **Customers** menu, pointing to **New**, and then clicking **New Credit Memo**.

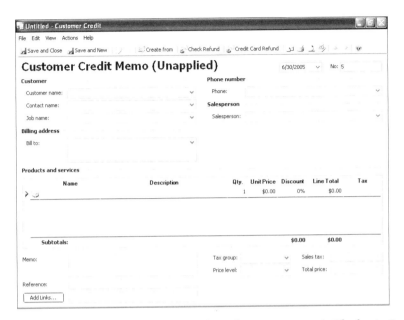

The credit memo you create depends on how you create it. The basic **Credit Memo** form assumes you will refund money the customer paid for goods or services. However, if you issue a refund for payment based on an invoice or for a job, you can save time by basing the credit memo on the invoice or job information stored in Small Business Accounting.

Handling Customer Returns

When you accept a return, you need to place the item back into your inventory. If the item is still in salable condition, you can add it to your inventory; however, if the item is no longer in brand-new condition or is in an open box, you will probably sell the item at a discount. Should the item be defective, you will be returning the item to the vendor from which you purchased it.

See Also For more information on adjusting inventory quantities and values, see Chapter 4, "Managing Products and Services." For more information on returning an item to a vendor, see Chapter 11, "Purchasing from and Paying Vendors."

Issuing a Refund by Check

When a customer purchases an item by check or cash, and in some cases when the customer pays by credit card, you will be able to write a company check for the amount of the refund. After you fill out the **Customer Credit** form, you can click the **Check Refund** button at the top of the form to create a new check for the amount of the refund.

Note This exercise assumes that you created the cash sale transaction for Katie Jordan earlier in this chapter.

In this exercise, you will create a check to refund a customer's purchase price.

OPEN the Fabrikam sample file if you have closed it.

1 On the **Customers** menu, point to **New,** and then click **New Credit Memo.**

A blank **Customer Credit Memo** form appears.

2 Click the **Customer Name** down arrow, and then click **Katie Jordan.**

3 In the **Products and Services** list, click in the **Name** column.

A down arrow appears.

4 In the **Name** column, click the down arrow, and then click **Electrical Materials (FF).**

5 On the **File** menu, click **Save.**

Small Business Accounting saves your credit memo.

6 On the **Customer Credit Memo** form toolbar, click **Check Refund.**

An untitled **Check** form appears.

7 Click the **Bank Account** down arrow, and then click **Checking.**

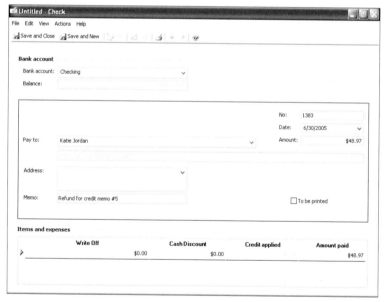

8 Click **Save and Close.**

Issuing a Refund by Credit Card

Because customers might have to pay interest on credit card purchases from the date of the purchase, it's good business practice to offer to transfer the amount of a return to the customer's credit card. The first part of issuing a refund to a customer's credit card is similar to issuing a refund by check, but the last steps depend on your credit card processing plan.

Important You must be signed up for a credit card processing plan to issue refunds to a customer's credit card.

In this exercise, you will refund a customer's money by crediting the amount of their purchase to their credit card.

OPEN the Northwind Traders sample file.

1 On the **Customers** menu, point to **New,** and then click **New Credit Memo.**

A blank **Customer Credit Memo** form appears.

2 Click the **Customer Name** down arrow, and then click **Alpine Ski House.**

3 In the **Products and Services** list, click in the first **Name** field.

A down arrow appears.

4 Click the **Name** down arrow, and then click **Snowboard, Freestyle.**

5 In the **Qty.** field, type 4.

6 On the **File** menu, click **Save.**

Small Business Accounting saves your credit memo.

7 On the **Customer Credit Memo** form toolbar, click **Credit Card Refund.**

8 Follow the instructions in the wizard to complete the refund.

Note The instructions you see depend on the credit card processing plan you selected.

Creating a Customer Credit Memo for a Job

When you work for a service-oriented company, you might be in the unfortunate position of being required to refund a customer's money for a job. If you build a deck that subsequently collapses, or if a customer decides to cancel a contract within the legally allowed time period, you will need to refund the money. Rather than manually create a credit memo that contains the individual line items from the job, you can create the credit memo based on the job itself.

In this exercise, you will create a customer credit memo for a job.

OPEN the Fabrikam sample file.

1 On the **Customers** menu, point to **Customer Lists,** and then click **Jobs.**

The **Job List** appears.

2   Double-click the **City Power & Light** job.

The **Workshop – Job** window appears.

3   On the **Actions** menu, click **New Credit Memo for This Job**.

A blank **Customer Credit Memo** form appears.

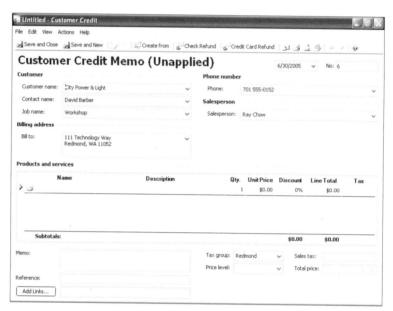

4   On the first row of the **Products and Services** list, click in the **Name** field.

A down arrow appears.

5   Click the **Name** field down arrow and then click **Framing/Finish Materials (FF)**.

6   In the **Qty.** field, type 3.

7   Click **Save and Close**.

Small Business Accounting saves your credit memo.

Creating a Customer Credit Memo from an Invoice

Just as you can create a credit memo based on a job's details, you can create a credit memo from an invoice. The process is quite similar; the only difference is that you display the invoice list and open the **Actions** menu to select the **Create Credit Memo** menu item.

In this exercise, you will create a credit memo based on an invoice.

OPEN the Fabrikam sample file if you have closed it.

1 On the **Customers** menu, point to **Customer Lists**, and then click **Invoices**.

The **Invoice List** appears.

2 Click invoice **1088**, the invoice for Jeff Low's solar sunroom.

3 On the **Actions** menu, click **Create Credit Memo**.

A **Customer Credit Memo** based on the selected invoice appears.

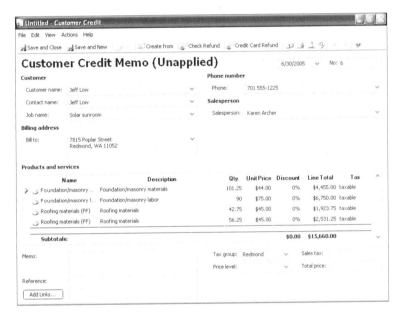

4 In the **Products and Services** list, right-click the first row header, and then click **Delete**.

The **Foundation/Mason Materials** item disappears.

5 Right-click the **Foundation/Masonry Labor** item's row header, and then click **Delete**.

6 Right-click the first **Roofing Materials (FF)** item, and then click **Delete**.

7 In the remaining row's **Qty.** field, type 5.

8 Click **Save and Close**.

Small Business Accounting saves your credit memo.

Designing Credit Memo Templates

Small Business Accounting includes a variety of Microsoft Office Word templates you can use to create your credit memos. The Word templates use the *Extensible Markup Language (XML)* to connect the data in your company file to fields in your Word documents. You can see a list of available data fields in the **Document Actions** task pane, at the right of the Word program window.

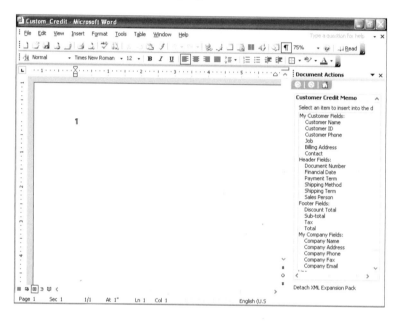

See Also For information on creating XML-based Word templates, see the section "Creating a Customer Statement Template" in Chapter 5, "Setting Up Customer Information."

Key Points

■ Small Business Accounting enables you to receive payments made by check, cash, or credit card.

■ You can't delete a payment after you have received it—you can only void the payment.

■ Managing refunds is vital to maintaining good customer relations. Learn how to handle refunds smoothly!

■ Create custom credit memo templates to reflect your business designs and identity.

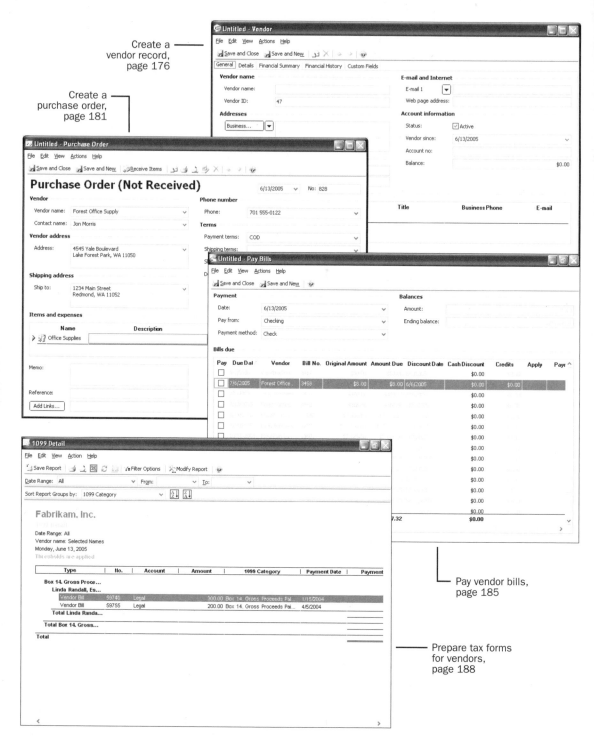

Create a vendor record,
page 176

Create a
purchase order,
page 181

Pay vendor bills,
page 185

Prepare tax forms
for vendors,
page 188

11 Purchasing from and Paying Vendors

In this chapter you will learn to:

✔ Create a vendor record.

✔ View the vendor list.

✔ Create a purchase order.

✔ Receive purchased items.

✔ Pay vendor bills.

✔ Prepare tax forms for vendors.

Vendors are the companies and individuals from whom you purchase goods and services. Legal fees, office supplies, contract labor, and inventory items are all examples of the kinds of services and materials you buy from vendors. Transactions with vendors affect the balances of the Accounts Payable account, your inventory account (if your business holds inventory), and expense accounts.

In Microsoft Office Small Business Accounting 2006, you often initiate a transaction with a vendor by creating a purchase order that specifies the items you are purchasing and the prices, discounts (if any), and payment terms that apply. As part of managing vendor transactions, you can enter a transaction that records your receipt of the goods and services you have purchased, and you can also set up vendor bills to pay when you receive related invoices.

In certain cases, you need to report the amounts you pay to a vendor for tax purposes. Many of these cases affect only businesses in special lines of work. For example, you need to report royalty payments as well as proceeds from the operation of a fishing boat. On the other hand, the compensation you pay to an individual who is not an employee— a graphic designer, a freelance marketer, or a carpenter, for example—also falls into this category, and many businesses have expenses such as these.

In this chapter, you'll first learn how to set up vendor records and how to work with the vendor list. You'll then learn how to create and manage purchase orders, item receipts, and vendor bills and how to compile the information you need to prepare tax forms for vendors.

See Also Do you need only a quick refresher on the topics in this chapter? See the Quick Reference entries on pages xxxiii–xxxiv.

Creating a Vendor Record

A vendor record contains contact information and details about the vendor's account. For example, on a vendor record you can specify the method a vendor uses most often to ship goods to you, the payment terms you have set up with a vendor, and the discount you typically receive on goods you purchase. In addition to contact information and account details, the form you use to create and view a vendor record includes **Financial Summary** and **Financial History** tabs. As you enter and process purchase orders and vendor bills, these tabs provide an overview of the status of the vendor's account. You can also use the entries on these tabs for quick access to vendor transactions.

From the **Vendors** home page, you can manage vendor information, initiate purchase orders, receive items into inventory, and enter and pay vendor bills. The **Vendors** home page also includes a **Spotlight** section that provides links to Web sites and online resources with information related to managing a small business.

Creating a New Vendor Record

When you want to purchase an item from a new vendor, you need to add that vendor's information to the vendor list. To add a vendor to your company file, open the **Vendors** menu, point to **New**, and then click **New Vendor**. A blank **Vendor** form appears.

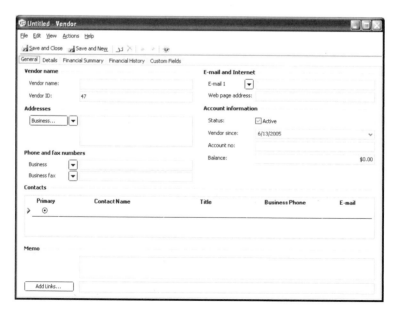

The **Vendor** form contains five tabs. When you first create a vendor record, you work mainly with the fields on the **General** and the **Details** tabs. You can use the **Custom Fields** tab on the vendor form to define your own fields in which to store vendor information. You can create text, date, number, and check box fields. The fields you create are not unique to a specific vendor—they appear on every vendor record.

Most of the form fields are self-evident, but the fields in the **Addresses, Phone and Fax Numbers**, and **E-mail and Internet** sections require some explanation because you can add more than one address, phone number, fax number, and e-mail address to each vendor's record. When you click the large down arrow button next to the **Business** label in the **Phone and Fax Numbers** section of the form, for example, Small Business Accounting displays a list that contains the items **Home, Business, Mobile, Assistant**, and **Other**. If you click **Mobile**, the **Business** label changes to **Mobile**, the **Business** number (if any) disappears, and you get a blank space into which you can type the vendor point of contact's mobile phone number.

If the vendor you're recording has an opening balance, such as a credit for signing up or an outstanding charge not transferred over from your previous accounting package, you type that value in the **Balance** field. After you save a vendor record in which you've entered an opening balance, the **Balance** field is no longer displayed on the vendor record form. The balance information appears in the **Balance Due** area of the **Financial Summary** tab.

You can organize the vendors you work with into groups. Vendor groups let you review vendor transactions in more detail, which helps you analyze your business more effectively. You can create a group for "Preferred" vendors, for example, and add to this group those vendors from whom you receive volume discounts. To create a vendor group, open the **Company** menu, point to **Manage Support Lists**, and then click **Vendor Group List**. You can then use the controls in the **Modify Vendor Group** dialog box to add, edit, or remove vendor groups.

In this exercise, you'll create a record for a vendor, set up a vendor group, and specify account details for a vendor.

OPEN the Fabrikam sample file.

1 On the **Navigation** pane, click **Vendors**.

   The **Vendors** home page appears.

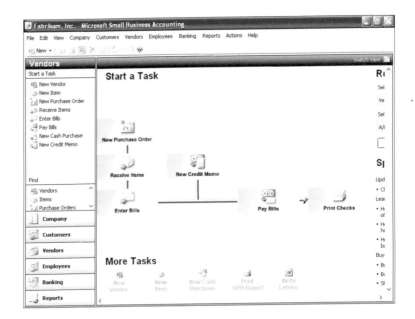

Tip   You can view the **Vendors** home page in the task flow view or in list view. To change the view, click **Switch View** in the upper right corner of the home page. The task flow view shows a typical series of steps in processing a vendor transaction. First you create a purchase order and send it to a vendor. When the items arrive, you can create an item receipt. When the vendor's invoice arrives, you enter the bill for payment. Keep in mind that you do not need to create a purchase order. You can start a vendor transaction anywhere along this path. For example, you can start by entering a vendor bill.

2   On the **Vendors** home page, under **More Tasks**, click **New Vendor**.

A blank **Vendor** form appears.

See Also   For detailed information about creating custom fields, see the section "Creating a Customer Record" in Chapter 5, "Setting Up Customer Information."

---

3   In the **Vendor Name** box, type David Jaffe.

4   Under **Addresses**, click **Business**.

5   In the **Address** dialog box, type 345 Elm St., Aberdeen, WA, 04121 into the **Street**, **City**, **State/Province**, and **Zip/Postal Code** fields.

Note   If your vendor list includes vendors from more than one country or region of the world, click **Add a New Country/Region** in the **Address** dialog box to build the list of locations. In addition to the name of the country or region, you can enter a country code that is based on standards set by the International Organization for Standardization (ISO). You can order the list of ISO codes at *www.iso.org*.

6 Under **Phone and Fax Numbers**, in the **Business** field, type (425) 555-0134.

7 In the **Account Information** area, keep the **Active** check box selected. Only active vendors are displayed by default in the vendor list.

8 In the **Vendor since** box, type 3/14/2005.

9 Under **Contacts**, in the **Contact Name** field, type David Jaffe, press [Tab], and then, in the **Title** field, type Sole Proprietor.

> **Tip** You can use the **Add Links** button on the **General** tab to assemble links to documents related to a vendor account. For example, you can create a link to a credit application you filled out to establish an account with a vendor, or a link to a proposal or budget that the vendor has submitted to you.

10 Click the **Details** tab.

The **Details** tab appears.

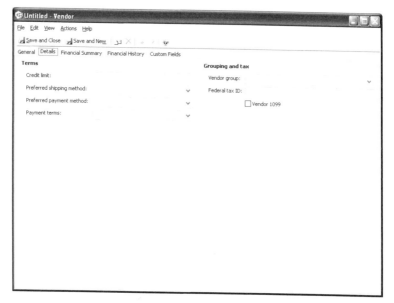

11 Under **Terms**, in the **Credit Limit** field, type 10000.

12 Under **Grouping and Tax**, in the **Vendor Group** list, click **Add a New Vendor Group**.

The **Vendor Group** dialog box appears.

13 In the **Vendor Group Name** field, type Preferred, and then click **OK**.

The **Vendor Group** dialog box disappears.

14 Select the **Vendor 1099** check box.

15 On the **Vendor** form, click **Save and Close**.

See Also For more information about 1099 tax forms for vendors, see the section "Preparing 1099 Forms for Vendors," later in this chapter. For information about the categories of vendor payments that affect 1099 tax reporting, on the **Company** menu, point to **Manage Support Lists**, and then click **1099 Category List**.

---

16 The **Vendor** form disappears.

> **Note** You can delete a vendor record if you have not recorded any transactions for that vendor and the vendor has no financial history in Small Business Accounting. If you have recorded transactions for a vendor, you can mark the vendor record inactive, but you cannot delete the record. A vendor record that is marked inactive is not displayed in vendor lists in dialog boxes or forms. To delete a vendor record from the vendor list, select the record, and then click **Delete** on the toolbar. To make a vendor record inactive, select the record in the vendor list, and then click **Make Inactive** on the **Edit** menu. You can change an inactive vendor's status back to active by selecting the vendor record in the vendor list and then clicking **Make Active** on the **Edit** menu.

Viewing the Vendor List

The vendor list provides a summary of contact information and shows the balance you owe to vendors. You can sort and filter the list to view a group of vendors or to see the record of a specific vendor. To display the vendor list, open the **Vendors** menu, point to **Vendor Lists**, and then click **Vendors**.

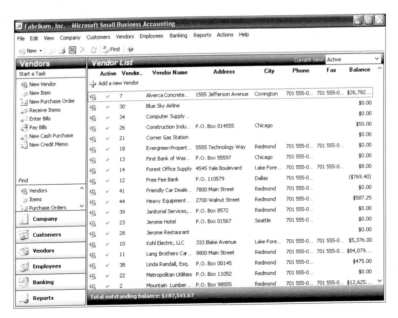

Creating a Purchase Order

You can use a purchase order to initiate and document a vendor transaction in which you buy inventory items or services that you need to run your business. You can send a purchase order to a vendor or simply use a purchase order as part of your company's internal accounting controls so that you can keep track of what and how much you have ordered.

A purchase order often serves as an authorization to place an order. For example, in addition to listing the items you are ordering and the price for each item, a purchase order specifies details such as payment terms, shipping terms, shipping methods, and delivery date.

To create a new purchase order, open the **Vendors** menu, point to **New**, and then click **New Purchase Order**. A new **Purchase Order** form appears.

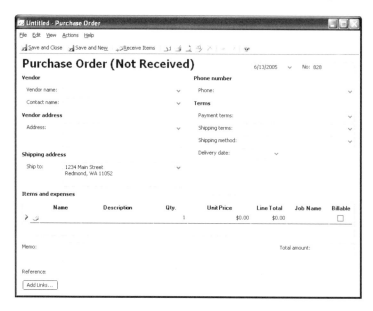

When you first create a purchase order, the status of the order is **Not Received**. Small Business Accounting fills in the current date and assigns a number to the purchase order. It also fills in the Ship To address. You can modify the date and the number if you need to. For example, you can change the number to conform to a purchase order numbering system that you have set up for your company or that matches the numbering system for a vendor.

You use the top portion of the purchase order form to enter vendor contact information and to specify the terms of the purchase order: when payment is due, whether you or the vendor pays for shipping, how the order should be shipped, and when the order is due.

In the **Items and Expenses** area of the form, you create the list of items the purchase order covers. Each line item shows the name and a description of the item, the quantity, unit price, and the line total. To add an item to an invoice, click in a blank row's **Name** field, click the down arrow that appears, and then click the item you want to add to the invoice. You can also create a new item by clicking **Add a New Item**, the first entry on the list that appears when you click the down arrow.

If your company preferences are set up to use jobs or classes, each line item includes a field for selecting a job or class name and a field for specifying whether an item you are ordering is billable. If an item is billable, you can bill a customer for the cost of this item later when you create an invoice.

When you have completed the list of line items for a purchase order, you can use the **Memo** box to provide a brief annotation about the order. You can use the **Reference** box to indicate an internal reference for your company or to add a reference number provided by the vendor. To link to a document that is related to this purchase order, click **Add Links** and then select the document in the **Select File To Link To** dialog box.

In this exercise, you'll create a purchase order for one of the vendors set up in the Fabrikam sample company.

Note This exercise illustrates a purchase order for office supplies, which are most often accounted for in an expense account. You can also create a purchase order for inventory items or for services.

OPEN the Fabrikam sample file if you have closed it.

1. On the **Vendors** menu, point to **New**, and then click **New Purchase Order**.

   A blank **Purchase Order** form appears.

2. Click the **Vendor Name** down arrow and then click **Forest Office Supply**.

3. In the **Payment Terms** field, click **1% 10 Net 30**.

4. In the **Shipping Method** field, click **Local Delivery**.

5. In the **Delivery date** field, select tomorrow's date.

   Note Shipping terms specify who will bear the cost for transporting an order. The cost of shipping is not a vital component of every purchase you place, but for orders that come from overseas or from other states or regions, whether you or the vendor is paying for shipping the goods makes a big difference. You might be responsible for paying freight charges before delivery or at the time of delivery, or the vendor will agree to pay the shipping costs. You compile the list of shipping terms you use by creating a support list in Small Business Accounting. To create the list, on the **Company** menu, point to **Manage Support Lists**, and then click **Shipping Term List**.

6 Under **Items and Expenses**, click the icon at the left of the first row, and then click **Expense**.

7 In the **Name** column, select account 6240, **Office Supplies**.

8 In the **Description** box, type Copier paper.

9 In the **Qty.** (quantity) field, type 100.

10 In the **Unit Price** field, enter $2.99.

When you fill in the **Unit Price** field, Small Business Accounting calculates the dollar value of the **Line Total** by multiplying **Unit Price** by **Qty**.

11 Repeat steps 8 through 10 to add a line item for Toner to the purchase order. In the **Qty.** field, type 12. In the **Unit Price** field, enter $15.50.

12 On the toolbar, click **Save and Close**.

Small Business Accounting records the purchase order, and the **Purchase Order** form disappears.

Note You can export a purchase order to Microsoft Office Word and then print the purchase order. In the Word document, you can add your company logo or other information before you print the purchase order. To export a purchase order, on the **Actions** menu, click **Export to Word**. In the **Select Word Templates** dialog box, select the template you want to use, and then click **Select**. You can also create your own template for a purchase order, just as you can for invoices, quotes, and other accounting documents. For detailed steps on creating a template, see the section "Creating a Quote Template" in Chapter 7, "Generating and Managing Quotes."

Receiving Purchased Items

The status of a purchase order can help you track the orders you place. For example, you can filter the list of purchase orders to see the orders that you have received and those that are still pending.

Sometimes you receive an order from a vendor before the vendor invoices you for the items you purchased. At other times, a vendor delivers only a portion of an order. In Small Business Accounting, you can create an item receipt so that items that you receive can be entered into your inventory or recorded as an expense. You can view item receipts on the **Bills and Item Receipts** list.

You can create an item receipt from scratch or directly from a purchase order. In the item receipt, you can verify that you received the full quantity of the items ordered or update the quantity received in the event a vendor sends a partial shipment.

When you receive items, the item receipt is posted to the Pending Item Receipts account and to the Inventory Asset account or the applicable expense account. When you enter the bill, the item receipt is removed from the Pending Item Receipts account and the Inventory or Expense account, and the bill is posted to Accounts Payable and the Inventory or Expense account.

Note When you save an item receipt, it is posted to your company's accounts. Because an item receipt affects accounting, you cannot delete it. If you need to redo an item receipt, you can edit it or void it.

By specifying a vendor name on the **Item Receipt** form before clicking **Create From**, you can filter the list of purchase orders in the **Select a Purchase Order** dialog box to show only purchase orders for the vendor you select. If you click **Create From** before you specify a vendor name, you will see a complete list of open purpose orders.

To help manage your receipt of a partial order, you can create more than one item receipt from a single purchase order. Small Business Accounting keeps track of the quantity ordered and the quantity received. When you create an item receipt from this purchase order again, the new purchase order would reflect the undelivered items.

For accounting purposes, the expense account is credited with the amount due only for the number of items you receive, not for the entire amount covered by the purchase order.

In this exercise, you will create and post an item receipt. You will base the item receipt on the purchase order for the office supplies that you created in the previous exercise.

OPEN the Fabrikam sample file.

1   On the **Navigation** pane, click **Vendors**.

2   On the **Vendors** home page, under **Start a Task**, click **Receive Items**.

A blank **Item Receipt** form appears.

3 In the **Vendor name** box, click Forest Office Supply.

4 On the **Actions** menu, click **Create From**.

The **Select a Purchase Order** dialog box.

5 Click the purchase order you created in the previous exercise, and then click **OK**.

6 In the line item for copier paper, change the value in the **Qty.** field from 100 to 60.

7 In the **Memo** field, type 40 units of copier paper on back order.

8 On the toolbar, click **Save and Close**.

Small Business Accounting records the items received into inventory, and the **Item Receipt** form disappears.

Invoices, Inventory, and Purchase Orders

You can see the need to keep up with your accounting paperwork in the relationship between customer invoices, inventory levels, and purchase orders. When you add a quantity of an item from your inventory to a customer invoice but don't have enough of that item in stock to fill the order, Small Business Accounting warns you of the shortage.

Paying Vendor Bills

To keep track of the amounts you owe to vendors, you need to enter bills into Small Business Accounting. You can enter the details of a bill from scratch by using an invoice or other paperwork the vendor provides, or you can create a bill from a purchase order or an item receipt that you created in Small Business Accounting.

The form you use to create a bill is similar to the purchase order and item receipt forms you worked with in exercises earlier in this chapter. In filling out the vendor bill form, you identify the vendor, specify payment terms, and enter details about the items being billed for. When you create a bill from a purchase order or an item receipt, the information in the source document is carried forward into the bill form. You can modify information in the bill (for example, updating payment terms if you are paying the bill early and qualify for a discount) or you can simply save the bill as is and pay it when you process your monthly checks.

If the bill you are preparing is related to a job that you have set up in Small Business Accounting, you can enter a job name for the line item and then select the **Billable** check box. An item that you mark Billable appears in the **Time and Materials** dialog box. You can then add this item to a customer's invoice. For more information about preparing invoices for a job, see the section "Creating an Invoice from a Quote or a Job," in Chapter 9, "Managing Invoices."

The accounts in the **Pay from** list are cash accounts, bank accounts, and credit card accounts that are included in your chart of accounts. If you select a credit card account, the amounts of the bills you choose to pay are added to the current liability for that account. If you select a cash account or a bank account such as Checking, the amounts of the bills are deducted from the balance of that account when the bills are paid.

The **Amount** box displays a running total of the amounts of the bills you select to pay. The **Balance** box initially shows the balance of the account you select in the **Pay from** list. As you select each bill to pay, the balance of this account is changed accordingly.

In this exercise, you will first enter a vendor bill from an item receipt. You will then follow the steps to select which vendor bills to pay.

OPEN the Fabrikam sample file if you have closed it.

1   On the **Navigation** pane, click **Vendors**.

    The **Vendors** home page appears.

2   Under **Start a Task**, click **Enter Bills**.

    A blank **Vendor Bill** form appears.

3   In the **Vendor Name** box, click **Forest Office Supply**.

4   On the form toolbar, click **Create From**.

    The **Select a Purchase Order or an Item Receipt** dialog box appears.

5   Click the item receipt you created in the previous exercise, and then click **OK**.

    The **Select a Purchase Order or an Item Receipt** dialog box disappears.

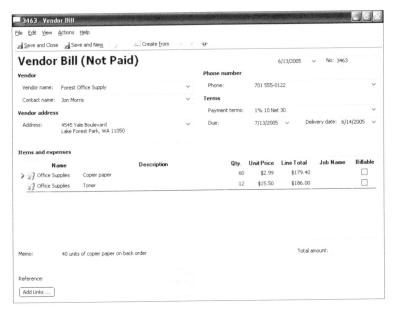

6 On the vendor bill form toolbar, click **Save and Close**.

The **Vendor Bill** window disappears.

7 On the **Vendors** home page, under **Start a Task**, click **Pay Bills**.

The **Pay Bills** window appears.

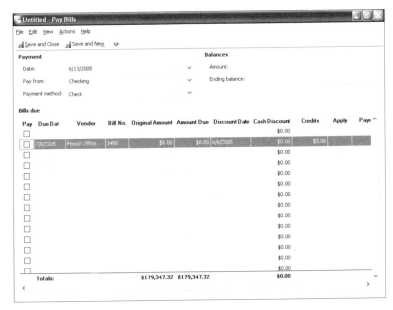

8 In the **Date** field, specify the date on which you are paying this batch of bills (if the date is not the current date).

9 In the **Pay from** list, click **Checking**.

10 In the **Payment Method** list, click **Check**.

11 In the **Pay** column, select the check box for each bill you want to pay.

12 Click **Save and Close**.

The **Pay Bills** window disappears.

Creating a Credit Memo

A credit memo is an accounting entry that you can apply to a vendor bill. For example, you might need to return a portion of an order to a vendor. You can create a credit memo from an unpaid bill, or if you have already paid for the order, you can create a credit memo that indicates the amount the vendor owes you. To enter the details for a credit memo, click **New Credit Memo** on the **Vendors** home page. When you select a bill to pay, the **Credits** button is displayed in the **Apply** column. Click this button to select the credit memo you want to apply.

Preparing 1099 Forms for Vendors

The 1099-MISC tax form is used to report certain kinds of income for United States federal income taxes. In some cases, a small business needs to prepare this form to report the amounts it has paid to a vendor. The 1099 form records the amounts you paid to the vendor during the previous tax year and the category to which the payments apply.

Most of the information you need to prepare 1099 forms comes from transactions that are recorded in one or another of your expense accounts. When you set up an expense account, you can indicate which 1099 category the account is related to. For example, in an expense account for legal fees, you can specify the 1099 category for amounts paid to an attorney.

Note The 1099 categories used in version 1.0 of Microsoft Office Small Business Accounting 2006 reflect the tax forms for 2004. You should be sure to check whether the categories have changed for later years.

Small Business Accounting includes two reports that you can use to help you prepare 1099-MISC tax forms for vendors. The 1099 Summary report shows you the total amount you have paid in each 1099 category. You can double-click a category listed in the 1099 Summary report to reveal detailed vendor records for each category. You can also run the 1099 Detail report directly.

Tip Remember that you don't need to prepare 1099 forms for all the vendors you work with. You prepare forms only for the vendors for which you select the 1099 Vendor check box on the vendor record form.

The 1099 Detail report is grouped by tax category. You can use the report as the basis for preparing the 1099-MISC forms for a particular tax year. Each vendor is listed along with detailed information about the amounts the vendor was paid. Only vendors for which you have checked the **1099 Vendor** option on the vendor record appear on this report.

You can filter the report by date range and by vendor name. By default, **Date Range** is set to show all 1099-related transactions. Other entries you can select from the **Date Range** list to filter the report include **This Month**, **This Fiscal Quarter**, and **This Fiscal Year**. You can also specify a custom time period by choosing dates in the **From** and **To** lists.

Tip After you filter the report to show the records for a specific vendor, you can print the report to use as a source for preparing the 1099-MISC tax form itself. To print the report, click **Print** on the **File** menu. You can also use commands on the **File** menu to export the report to Microsoft Office Excel or to save a filtered version of the report.

In this exercise, you will view and filter the 1099 Detail report that you can use to prepare tax forms for vendors.

1 On the **Navigation** pane, click **Vendors**.

2 On the **Vendors** home page, under **More Tasks**, click **Print 1099 Report**.

The **1099 Detail** report appears.

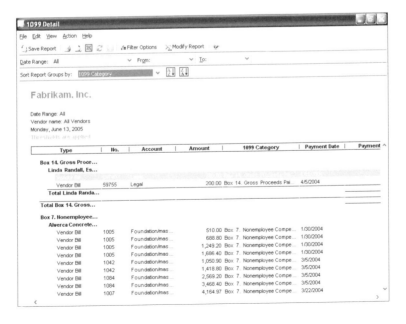

3 On the toolbar, click **Filter Options**.

The **Select Filter Options** dialog box appears.

4 Under **Select Filter Options**, click **Vendor Name**.

5 Under **Filter Options**, in the **Vendor Name** list, click **Selected Names**.

The **Select Names** dialog box appears.

6 Under **Available Options**, scroll down to see the list of vendors.

7 Click **Linda Randall, Esq.**, and then click **Add**.

8 In the **Select Names** dialog box, click **OK**, and then click **OK** in the **Select Filter Options** dialog box.

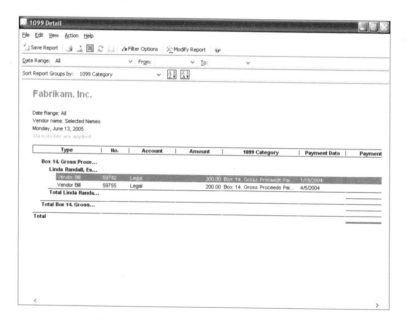

Key Points

- Vendors are the companies and individuals from whom you order supplies and inventory.

- Vendor transactions are documented through purchase orders, item receipts, and vendor bills.

- You don't need to create a purchase order for every vendor transaction. You can initiate a vendor transaction by entering a bill or by creating an item receipt.

- For some vendors, you need to prepare a 1099-MISC tax form to report the amounts you have paid them during the tax year.

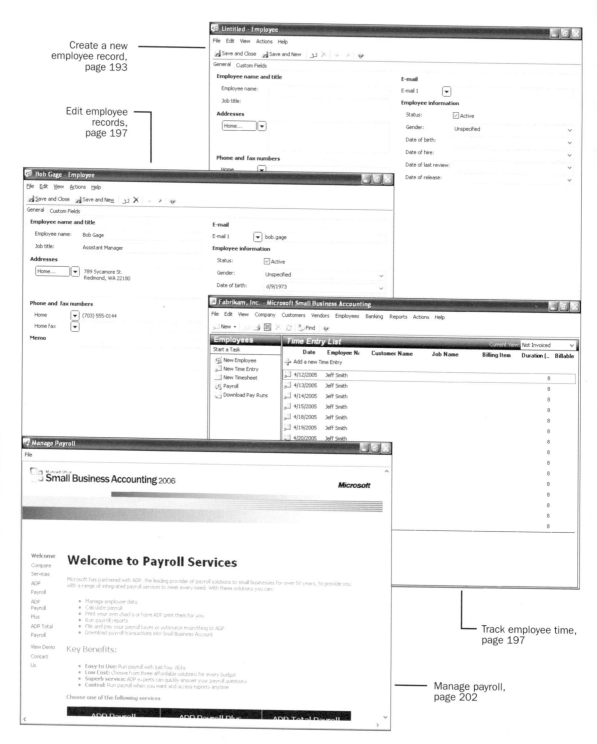

Create a new
employee record,
page 193

Edit employee
records,
page 197

Track employee time,
page 197

Manage payroll,
page 202

12 Managing Employee Time and Payroll

In this chapter you will learn to:

✔ Create new employee records.

✔ Edit employee records.

✔ Track employee time.

✔ Manage payroll.

Employees are the backbone of any business. Even if you only have one employee, yourself, it's your knowledge and time that make the business go. Tracking your employees' work throughout the week is essential to both accurate customer billing and correct payments to your employees. In this chapter, you will learn how to create and edit employee records, track employee time, and manage your company's payroll.

See Also Do you need only a quick refresher on the topics in this chapter? See the Quick Reference entries on page xxxiv.

Managing Employee Records

In Microsoft Office Small Business Accounting 2006, you manage your employee records by using the **Employees** home page, which you can display by clicking **Employees** in the **Navigation** pane.

The **Employees** home page contains entries for standard tasks such as entering new employee records, recording employee time, and running payroll, but you don't have to use the **Employees** home page to initiate those tasks. If you prefer, you can also start those processes from the **Employees** menu.

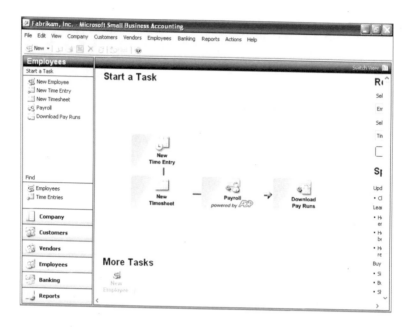

Creating New Employee Records

After you hire an employee, you need to enter that individual's information into Small Business Accounting so you can record work done by the new employee, add that person to your payroll system, and pay the employee for time worked. To create a new employee record, open the **Employees** menu and click **New Employee**. A blank **Employee** form appears.

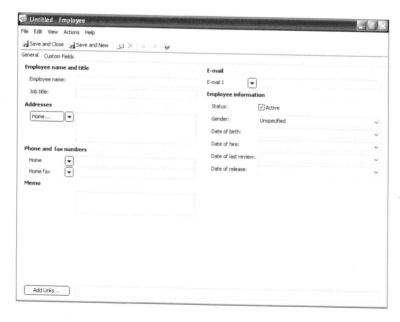

Most of the form fields are self-evident, but the fields in the **Addresses**, **Phone and Fax Numbers**, and **E-mail** sections require some explanation. You can actually add more than one address, phone number, fax number, and e-mail address to each employee's record. When you click the large down arrow button next to the **Home** label in the **Phone and Fax Numbers** section of the form, for example, Small Business Accounting displays a list that contains the items **Home**, **Business**, **Mobile**, **Assistant**, and **Other**. If you click **Mobile**, the **Home** label changes to **Mobile**, the **Home** number (if any) disappears, and you get a blank space into which you can type the employee's mobile phone number.

In this exercise, you will add a new employee record to the Fabrikam sample database.

OPEN the Fabrikam sample file.

1   On the **Employees** menu, click **New Employee**.

An untitled **Employee** form appears.

2   In the **Employee Name** field, type Bob Gage.

3   In the **Job Title** field, type Assistant Manager.

4   In the **Address** field, type 789 Sycamore St., Redmond, WA 22180.

5   In the **Phone and Fax Numbers** section, in the field currently labeled **Home**, type (703) 555-0144.

6   Click the down arrow next to the **Home** field, and click **Mobile**.

The **Home** field label changes to **Mobile**.

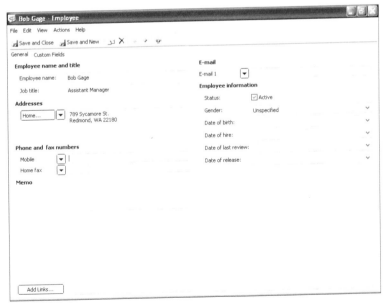

7   In the field now labeled **Mobile**, type (403) 555-0110.

8   In the **E-mail** section, in the field labeled **E-mail 1**, type bob.gage.

9   Click the **Gender** down arrow and then click **Male**.

10   In the **Date of Birth** field, type 8/9/1973.

11   In the **Date of Hire** field, type 4/14/2005.

12   In the **Date of Last Review** field, type 10/14/2005.

13   Click **Save and Close**.

Small Business Accounting saves your employee record.

Viewing and Manipulating the Employee List

Small Business Accounting groups all of your employee records into a single list, the employee list. To display the employee list, open the **Employees** menu, point to **Employee Lists**, and then click **Employees**.

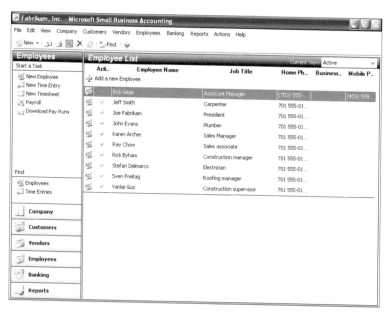

You can edit an employee's information by double-clicking the appropriate record in the list or add a new employee record by clicking the **Add a New Employee** item just below the list's header row.

See Also   For more information on sorting, filtering, and searching in a list, see the section "Viewing the Item List" in Chapter 4, "Managing Products and Services."

Editing Employee Records

Employees move, change phone numbers, and get new e-mail addresses, so you need to be able to edit their records to reflect their new contact information. If you do need to edit an employee's record, you can display the employee list, double-click the record you want, and make the edits in the **Employee** form that appears.

In this exercise, you will edit the employee record you created earlier in this chapter for Bob Gage.

OPEN the Fabrikam sample file if you have closed it.

1   On the **Employees** menu, point to **Employee Lists**, and then click **Employees**.

The **Employee List** appears.

2   Double-click the list record for **Bob Gage**.

The **Employee** form for **Bob Gage** appears.

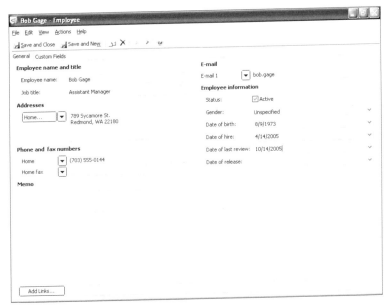

3   In the **Date of Last Review** field, type 11/14/2005.

4   Click **Save and Close**.

Small Business Accounting saves the edited employee record.

Tracking Employee Time

As a small business owner, you must pay close attention to how your employees allocate their time. Not only do you need to record their time so you know what work is getting done, but also you need to use your employees' time records to bill your clients for the labor it took to complete their projects.

Making a Single Time Entry

Employees can enter their time into Small Business Accounting themselves, or you can have them submit a separate time card and either you or an administrative assistant can enter their hours worked into the program. When employees need to make a single entry, they can add their time into the time entry list by opening the **Employees** menu and clicking **New Time Entry** to display a blank **Time Entry** form.

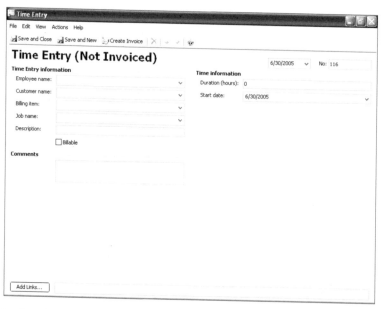

In the **Time Entry** form, you can select the employee's name, the name of the customer (if any) for whom the work was done, the billing item (an item from your item list), the job name (if any), and whether the time can be billed to the customer. The right side of the **Time Entry** form contains fields for you to enter the hours worked and the date the work began. When you're done creating the time entry, click **Save and Close** to record it in Small Business Accounting.

Editing a Time Entry

If you or an employee makes a mistake while making a time entry, you can display the time entry list, open the form that contains the time entry, edit the information, and save it. To edit a time entry, open the **Employees** menu, point to **Employee Lists**, and then click **Time Entries**. The **Time Entry List** appears.

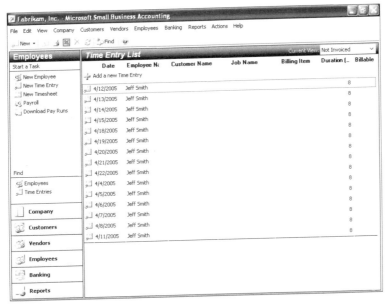

Double-click the time entry you want to edit to display it in a **Time Entry** form, make your changes, and then click **Save and Close** to record them.

See Also For more information on sorting, filtering, and searching in lists, see the section "Viewing the Item List" in Chapter 4, "Managing Products and Services."

Making Multiple Time Entries by Using a Timesheet

Recording single time entries is fine for part-time employees or contractors, but regular employees who put in 40 or more hours a week will probably want to enter a week's worth of time at once. In Small Business Accounting, employees can enter time for a week in a timesheet. To display a timesheet, open the **Employees** menu and click **New Timesheet**. A blank **Weekly Timesheet** form appears.

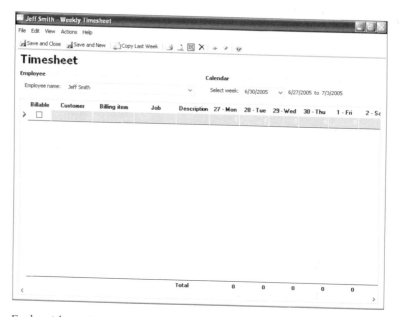

Each grid row in a timesheet is roughly equivalent to a **Time Entry** form. You can select whether the hours are billable to a client, the work you did, how many hours you spent on a project, and on which day you worked those hours. The **Timesheet** form summarizes your hours for you, displaying both daily and weekly hour totals.

Important   Resist the temptation to wait until the end of the week to record your hours! It's too easy to forget what you did and potentially bill the wrong client.

In this exercise, you will enter an employee's billable hours for a day by using a timesheet, add an entry by using the time entry list, and then edit a time entry.

Caution   The dates you enter into a **Timesheet** or **Time Entry** form must be in your company's current fiscal year. If Small Business Accounting won't accept the dates listed in the following exercise steps, change the dates so that they are in your company's current fiscal year.

OPEN the Fabrikam sample file if you have closed it.

1   On the **Employees** menu, click **New Timesheet**.

An untitled **Weekly Timesheet** form appears.

2   In the **Select Week** field, type 6/20/2005.

The dates in the time sheet change to reflect the week that begins on 6/20/2005.

3   Click the **Employee Name** down arrow and then click **Jeff Smith**.

4   In the first row of the grid, select the **Billable** check box.

5   Click in the **Customer** field, click the down arrow that appears, and then click **Alpine Ski House**.

6   Press the ⌨Tab key.

7   Click the **Billing Item** down arrow, and then click **Carpentry (TM)**.

8   Press ⌨Tab twice to move the insertion point to the **Description** field.

9   Type Emergency roof repair and then press ⌨Tab to move the insertion point to the **Monday** field.

10   Type 8 and press ⌨Tab to move to the next field.

11   Repeat the previous step three times to record eight hours of work for Tuesday, Wednesday, and Thursday of the current week.

The calculated entries in the **Total** row at the bottom of the grid change to reflect your entries.

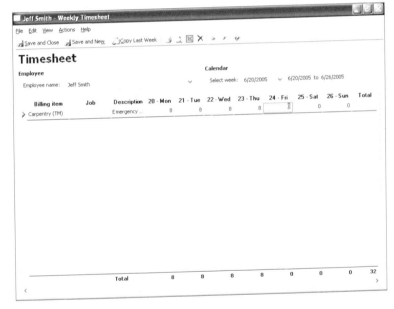

12   Click **Save and Close**.

Small Business Accounting saves the timesheet, closes it, and writes its contents to the time entry list.

13   On the **Employees** menu, point to **Employee Lists**, and then click **Time Entries**.
The **Time Entry List** appears.

14   Just below the **Time Entry List** headers, click **Add a New Time Entry**.
A **Time Entry** form appears.

15   Click the **Employee Name** field, and then click **Jeff Smith**.

16   Click the **Customer Name** down arrow, and then click **Alpine Ski House**.

17   Click the **Billing Item** down arrow, and then click **Carpentry (TM)**.

18   Select the **Billable** check box.

19   In the **Duration (hours)** field, type 9.

20   In the **Start Date** field, type 6/24/2005.

21   Click **Save and Close**.
Small Business Accounting saves your entry and displays the **Time Entry List**.

22   Double-click the time entry for 6/24/2005.
The entry appears in a **Time Entry** form.

23   In the **Duration (hours)** field, type 8.

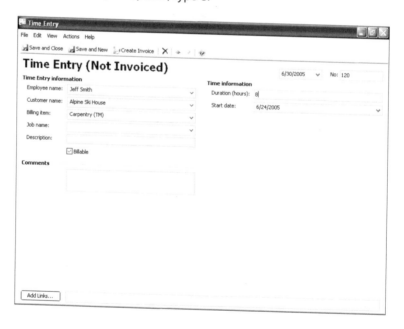

24 Click **Save and Close**.

Small Business Accounting saves your entry and displays the **Time Entry List**.

Managing Payroll

Managing your company's payroll requires you to write checks, calculate taxes and deductions, and file reports with the appropriate tax authorities. You can handle these tasks yourself, or you can outsource the payroll functions to an online service. This section shows you how to perform the necessary tasks under either scenario.

Outsourcing Payroll Processing

Handling payroll requirements takes time and energy. If you would like to delegate the responsibility of handling your payroll, you can take advantage of the built-in Small Business Accounting partnership with Automatic Data Processing, Inc. (ADP).

Warning If you selected the **Log Online Activities** check box on the **General** tab of the **Company Preferences** dialog box, the Small Business Accounting log file might contain sensitive items such as employee salary, address, and other personally identifiable information. The log file is stored in the My Documents\Small Business Accounting\Logs folder of the administrator who installed Small Business Accounting. In general, you should not make this log file available to anyone except the administrator, the business owner, and anyone with auditing responsibilities.

In this exercise you will sign up for ADP payroll processing.

OPEN a company file other than the two sample files that came with Small Business Accounting. You can't get into the online payroll sign-up process from a sample company file.

1 On the **Employees** menu, point to **Online Payroll**, and then click **Sign Up for Payroll Service**.

The ADP Payroll Web page appears.

2   Click the button representing the plan to which you want to subscribe.

3   Follow the instructions on the Web page to sign up for ADP online payroll processing.

4   When you are done, click the **Close** button to return to Small Business Accounting.

Downloading Payroll Information

AOne benefit of the integration between Small Business Accounting and ADP payroll processing is that you can download ADP payroll records into Small Business Accounting as a series of journal entries. As you view your payroll records on the ADP system, you'll be able to group the records by employee or company. You'll have to check your ADP account information to learn the full range of possibilities.

Note   The journal entries contain pay type information that you can view in the Transaction Detail by Account report. After you download payroll for the first time, Small Business Accounting will make the **Pay Type** field available in the **Time Entry** form and in timesheets.

BE SURE TO have your ADP payroll account user ID and password at hand. You also need to be connected to the Internet to download your payroll information.

In this exercise, you will download payroll information from ADP.

OPEN the Fabrikam sample file if you closed it earlier.

1 In the **Navigation Pane**, click **Employees**.

The **Employees** home page appears.

2 Under **Start a Task**, click **Download Pay Runs**.

The **Download Pay Runs** page appears.

3 Follow the instructions in the **Download Pay Runs** page.

4 Click **Save and Close**.

Small Business Accounting saves your payroll records as journal entries.

Doing Payroll Yourself

You can take advantage of a subscription payroll service, but if you would rather handle payroll yourself, you can do so by writing checks to your employees and to the tax authorities to whom you owe payments. It's a bit more work than processing the checks and payments through an online service, but you won't have to pay the subscription and processing fees.

First, you need to ensure that you have the correct accounts to which you can assign your payroll expenses. The Fabrikam sample company file comes with correct payroll accounts.

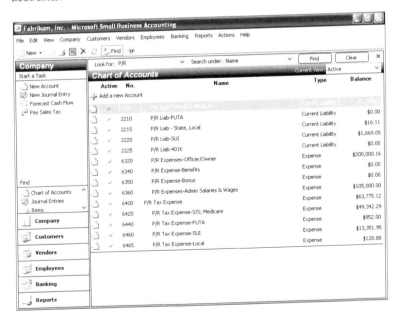

When you create a company by using the Startup Wizard, Small Business Accounting creates a series of accounts you can use to record the business owner's wages and benefits, plus a separate series of accounts you can use to record employee wages, bonuses, and benefits. If you didn't choose to create those accounts, or if you deleted them (perhaps anticipating you would never hire any employees), you can always create the accounts that you need.

The following table lists the available payroll accounts and describes when you should use them.

Account	Account Type	When to Use
Wages	Expense	If you write paychecks
Federal Tax	Current Liability	To record your federal tax liability
State Tax	Current Liability	If your payroll is subject to state taxes
Local Tax	Current Liability	If your payroll is subject to local taxes
Unemployment	Current Liability	If your payroll is subject to an unemployment fee

See Also If you pay your employees bonuses or overtime, you should add Expense subaccounts for those specific wage types. For more information on creating new accounts, see Chapter 3, "Managing the Chart of Accounts and Journal Entries List."

In this exercise you will process payroll checks manually.

OPEN the Fabrikam sample file.

1   On the **Banking** menu, click **Write Checks**.

A blank **Check** form appears.

2   Verify that **Checking** appears in the **Bank Account** field.

3   Click the **Pay to** down arrow, and then click **Joe Fabrikam**.

4   In the **Amount** field, type 4167.67, and press [Tab].

The amount appears as words in the unnamed field below the **Pay to** field.

5   In the **Items and Expenses** list, click in the first **Name** field.

A down arrow appears.

6   Click the **Name** down arrow and then click **6320 P/R Expenses-Officer/Owner**.

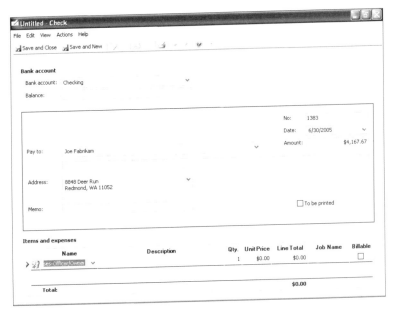

7   Click **Save and Close**.

Small Business Accounting saves your check, which you can fill out by hand
or print later.

Key Points

- Enter your employees into Small Business Accounting so you can start tracking
  their time and payroll information.

- You and your employees can create individual time entries in the time entry list or
  use timesheets to fill in an entire week on one form.

- When you write payroll checks for yourself and your employees, be sure to create
  entries for any taxes you owe on those salaries.

- If you don't have the time to handle payroll information manually, consider
  signing up for online processing through ADP or another service.

Glossary

account   A record of financial transactions, usually grouped around a particular category that helps financial planners determine deductible expenses and taxable income. For example, you would track the cost of professional association memberships, journal subscriptions, and research materials in the Dues, Publications, Books account.

account register   A list of transactions for a specific financial account.

accounting   The process of recording, classifying, summarizing, reporting, and assessing a company's business transactions. The goal of accounting is to maintain a detailed and accurate picture of the company's performance and health.

accounts payable   An account that contains records of monies you owe to your vendors. The Small Business Accounting program calculates this account's values from transactions you enter.

accounts receivable   An account that contains records of monies owed to your company for the sale of products and services. The Small Business Accounting program calculates this account's values from transactions you enter.

asset   A resource that the corporation owns, such as cash, inventory, or equipment.

back order   A reference to an item which a customer has ordered but which you do not currently have in stock.

balance sheet   A financial statement that summarizes your company's status on a specific date.

cash flow statement   A report that describes the amount of money a company expects to have on hand over a period of time.

chart of accounts   The list of your company's accounts and their balances.

credit   An entry on the right side of an account; debits are on the left. How a credit affects your bottom line depends on the type of account to which it is applied. A credit increases liabilities, equity, or income and decreases assets or expenses.

debit   An entry on the left side of an account; credits are on the right. How a debit affects your bottom line depends on the type of account to which it is applied. A debit increases assets or expenses and decreases liabilities, equity, or income.

depreciation   The amount of value that a physical item, such as a computer or automobile, is assumed to lose over time.

double-entry bookkeeping   An accounting method where transactions are represented as a credit to one account and debit from another account.

expense   An amount spent on products or services related to your normal business operations, such as utilities or wages.

fixed fee job   A job undertaken for a set price.

income   Revenue generated by selling products and services to your customers.

invoice   A request for payment you send to a customer.

item   A product or service your company offers for sale.

job   A multi-part project made up of products and services you deliver over time.

journal entry   A record of a transaction entered into an account register.

kit   A set of items sold as a single unit.

liability   A debt. Something owed, such as accounts payable or income taxes to be paid at a later date.

payment terms   The conditions under which customers are expected to pay for products and services.

profit and loss statement   A detailed statement that describes a company's performance over a period of time. A profit and loss statement usually starts with revenues and then covers expenses, but it goes into detail regarding expenses such as the cost of goods sold, operating expenses, taxes, loan interest, and other costs of doing business.

progress invoice   A request for payment for a partially-completed job.

quote   A document that specifies the products and services you agree to sell or provide to a customer, what those items will cost, and the delivery date of a proposed transaction.

report   A summary of specific information recorded in Small Business Accounting.

sales order   A record of a customer's request to purchase an item you offer for sale.

sales tax code   An entry that reflects the tax an authority levies on a transaction.

support list   A list Small Business Accounting creates to track customers, items, and other important business data.

time and materials job   A job where the customer will be billed for actual time and material expenses incurred while performing the job.

user account   A user name and password combination that allows employees to enter and view data in Small Business Accounting.

vendor   A company or individual from which you purchase products or services.

XML (Extensible Markup Language)   A text encoding standard that enables you to store data about a document's contents within that document.

Index

NOTE: Items with roman numerals refer to the Quick Reference pages at the front of the book. Page numbers with the preface *B* refer to pages in the two bonus chapters on the CD-ROM, Chapters 13 and 14.

Symbols

.log files, 21
.sbb files, 21
.sbc files, 21
.sbd files, 21
.sbl files, 21
.xml files, 21
.zip files, 21
1099-MISC tax form, 188
1099s
    category list, 40
    Detail report, 189

A

A/P Aging Summary report, 9
account registers, 47, B209
    sorting, B210
    viewing, xix, 47
Accountant role, 25
accounting, 2
    definition, 2
    duties, 3
accounts
    accounts payable, 34
    accounts receivable, 34
    asset, 33
    balance sheet, 32
    bank charge, 35
    cash discount given, 35
    cash discount taken, 35
    changing status, 49
    chart of, 32
    creating, xviii, 38
    customer, 45
    defined, 2
    deleting, 49
    editing, xviii, 38

equity, 33
    financial, 45
    income and expense, 32, 33
    inventory asset, 33
    liability, 33
    making inactive, 49
    merging, xviii, 42
    opening balances, 34
    pending item receipts, 35
    retained earnings, 35
    sales tax payable, 35
    subaccounts, 38
    system, 32, 34
    tax code, 45
    transferring funds, B217
    types, 32
    undeposited funds, 35
    vendor, 45
    write off, 35
Accounts Payable account, 34
Accounts Receivable account, 34
Add or Edit Item Group Name
    dialog box, xxiii
Add/Remove Reminders dialog
    box, 142
adding accounts to the chart of
    accounts, 38
adding and editing accounts,
    38–43
adding items to invoices, 147
adding line items to quotes, 119
ADP Payroll for Small Business
    Accounting service, 14
assets
    bank accounts, 33
    cash accounts, 33
    defined, 3
    fixed, 33
Automatic Data Processing, Inc.
    (ADP), 203

B

back orders, xxix, 141–143
    about, 141
    managing, 141
    partial invoices, 142
    setting reminders, 142
backing up, xvi, 22
    company data files, 22
    restoring data, 23
Backup dialog box, 23
balance sheets
    defined, 3
    purpose, 3
Bank Charge account, 35
bank deposits, B215–217
    Deposit form, B216
    deposit transactions, B215
    depositing from a vendor, B217
    recording, B215
Bank Fee dialog box, B213
bank fees, B213
Bank Interest dialog box, B212
banking, B209–226
    adding transactions, xxxv, B209,
        B210
    bank fees, B213
    online, B209
    reconciling, xxxvi, B220
    recording deposits, xxxvi, B215
bills
    entering, 186
    modifying, 186
    paying, 185
    paying online, B226
    vendor bill form, 186
Bills and Item Receipts list, 184
bills. *See also* invoices
Business Services, 15

Curtis Frye

Curtis Frye is a freelance writer from Portland, Oregon. He is the author of five books from Microsoft Press: *Microsoft Office Excel 2003 Step By Step*, *Microsoft Access 2002 Plain & Simple*, *Microsoft Excel 2002 Plain & Simple*, *Microsoft Excel 2002 Step By Step*, and *Faster Smarter Home Networking*. He also contributed six chapters to *Microsoft Office v. X for Mac Inside Out*. He's written several other books and online courses on Microsoft technologies, programming, and privacy-enhancing technologies.

Before beginning his writing career in June 1995, Curt spent four years with The MITRE Corporation as a defense trade analyst and one year as Director of Sales and Marketing for Digital Gateway Systems, an Internet service provider. Curt graduated from Syracuse University in 1990 with an honors degree in political science. When he's not writing, Curt is a professional improvisational comedian with ComedySportz.

Acknowledgments

Creating a book is a time-consuming (sometimes all-consuming) process, but working within an established relationship makes everything go much more smoothly. In that light, I'd like to thank my co-author, John Pierce, who took on a significant chunk of the book in addition to his usual duties at Microsoft. I'd also like to thank Juliana Aldous Atkinson, the acquisitions editor, for inviting me back for another tilt at the windmill; Sandra Haynes, for her editorial development help; and Valerie Wooley for her fine herding instincts, which kept us on track and moving forward.

I'd also like to thank Steve Sagman of Studioserv, who served as technical editor, production coordinator, and all-around great guy. Juliana touted his group as one of Microsoft's best packagers, and they all lived up to their reputation. Gail Taylor provided a thorough copy edit, changing what needed to be changed and asking insightful questions that improved the manuscript immensely.

Finally, none of this would have happened without the hard work of my agent, Neil Salkind, of Studio B Productions. His efforts, plus those of David and Sherry Rogelberg, the founders of Studio B, make it easy for me to make a living doing what I love.

What do you think of this book?
We want to hear from you!

Do you have a few minutes to participate in a brief online survey? Microsoft is interested in hearing your feedback about this publication so that we can continually improve our books and learning resources for you.

To participate in our survey, please visit:
www.microsoft.com/learning/booksurvey

And enter this book's ISBN, 0-7356-2154-3. As a thank-you to survey participants in the United States and Canada, each month we'll randomly select five respondents to win one of five $100 gift certificates from a leading online merchant.* At the conclusion of the survey, you can enter the drawing by providing your e-mail address, which will be used for prize notification *only*.

Thanks in advance for your input. Your opinion counts!

Sincerely,

Microsoft Learning

Learn More. Go Further.